PENELOPE RIDES AGAIN

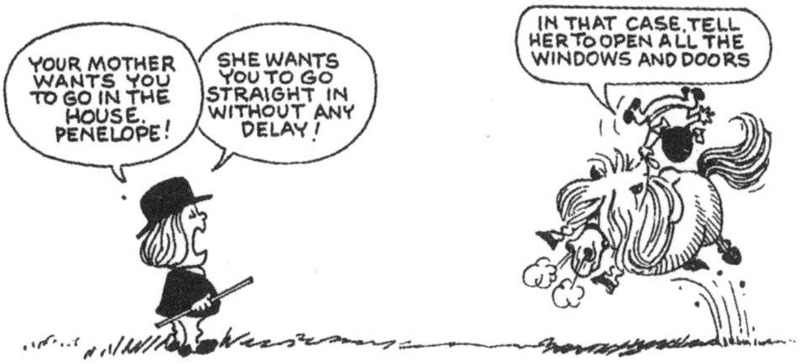
YOUR MOTHER WANTS YOU TO GO IN THE HOUSE, PENELOPE!
SHE WANTS YOU TO GO STRAIGHT IN WITHOUT ANY DELAY!
IN THAT CASE, TELL HER TO OPEN ALL THE WINDOWS AND DOORS

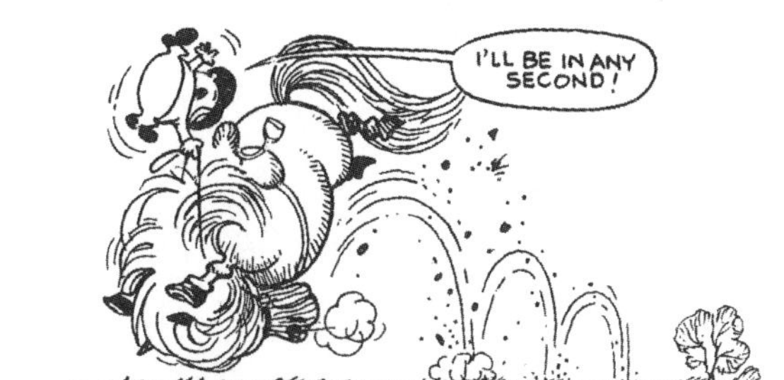
I'LL BE IN ANY SECOND!

also by Norman Thelwell

ANGELS ON HORSEBACK
THELWELL COUNTRY
THELWELL IN ORBIT
A LEG AT EACH CORNER
A PLACE OF YOUR OWN
TOP DOG
THREE SHEETS IN THE WIND
UP THE GARDEN PATH
THE COMPLEAT TANGLER
THELWELL'S BOOK OF LEISURE
THE EFFLUENT SOCIETY
PENELOPE
BELT UP
THIS DESIRABLE PLOT
THELWELL'S BRAT RACE
THELWELL'S GYMKHANA
THELWELL GOES WEST
THELWELL'S PONY CAVALCADE
A PLANK BRIDGE BY A POOL
A MILLSTONE ROUND MY NECK
SOME DAMN FOOL'S SIGNED THE RUBENS AGAIN
THELWELL'S MAGNIFICAT
THELWELL'S SPORTING PRINTS
WRESTLING WITH A PENCIL
PLAY IT AS IT LIES
THELWELL'S PONY PANORAMA

thelwell's

PENELOPE RIDES AGAIN

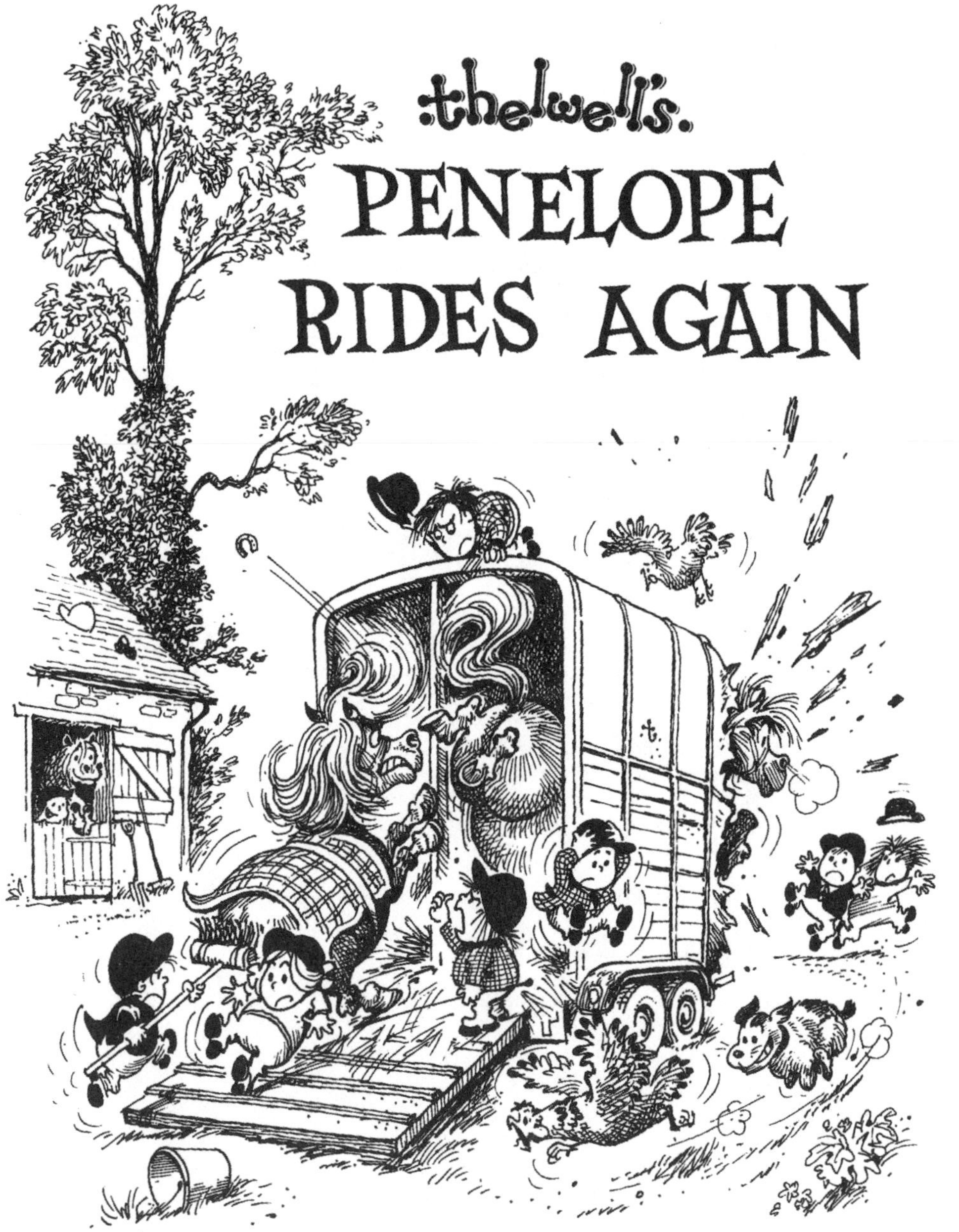

TRAFALGAR SQUARE
North Pomfret, Vermont

This edition published in the United States of America in 2022 by
Trafalgar Square Books
North Pomfret, Vermont 05053

Originally published in Great Britain in 1989 by Methuen Publishing Limited, York

Disclaimer of Liability
The author and publisher shall have neither liability nor responsibility to any person
or entity with respect to any loss or damage caused or alleged to have been caused
directly or indirectly by the information contained in this book. While the book is as
accurate as the author can make it, there may be errors, omissions, and inaccuracies.

Trafalgar Square Books encourages the use of approved safety helmets in all
equestrian sports and activities.

Library of Congress Control Number: 2022936307
ISBN: 978-1-64601-169-8

Cover design by RM Didier

Printed in the United States of America

10 9 8 7 6 5 4 3 2 1

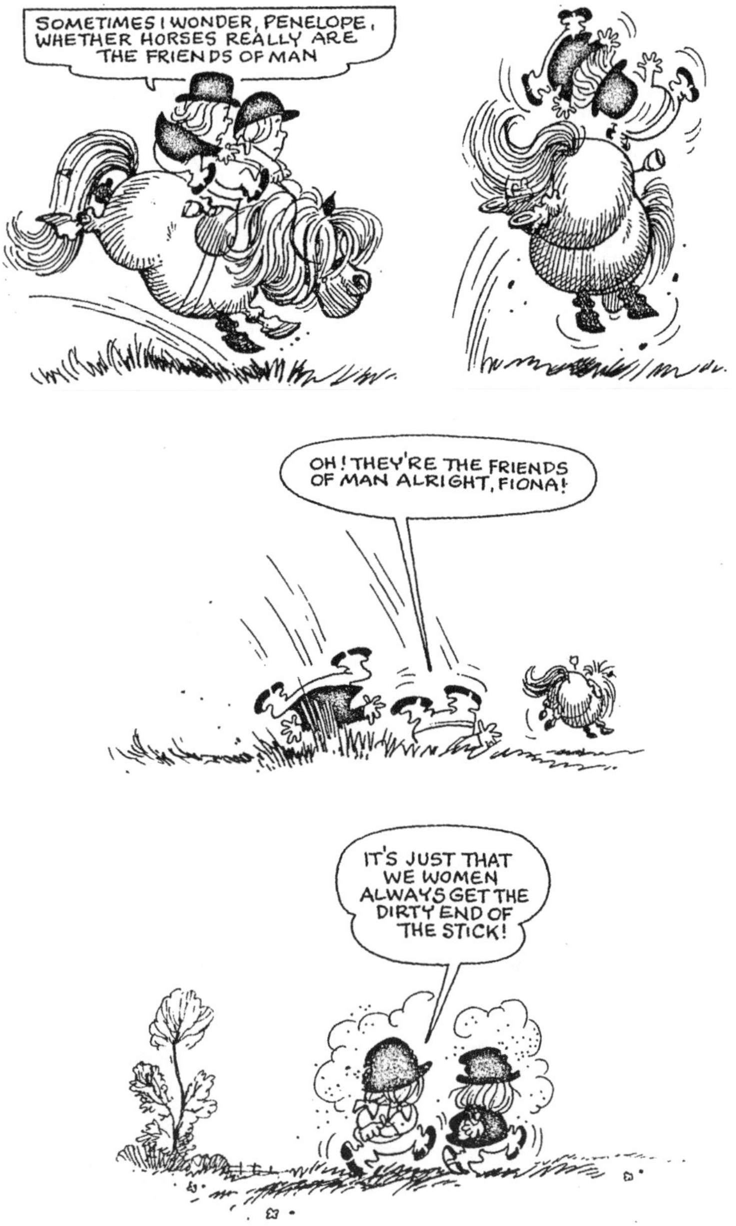
SOMETIMES I WONDER, PENELOPE, WHETHER HORSES REALLY ARE THE FRIENDS OF MAN
OH! THEY'RE THE FRIENDS OF MAN ALRIGHT, FIONA!
IT'S JUST THAT WE WOMEN ALWAYS GET THE DIRTY END OF THE STICK!

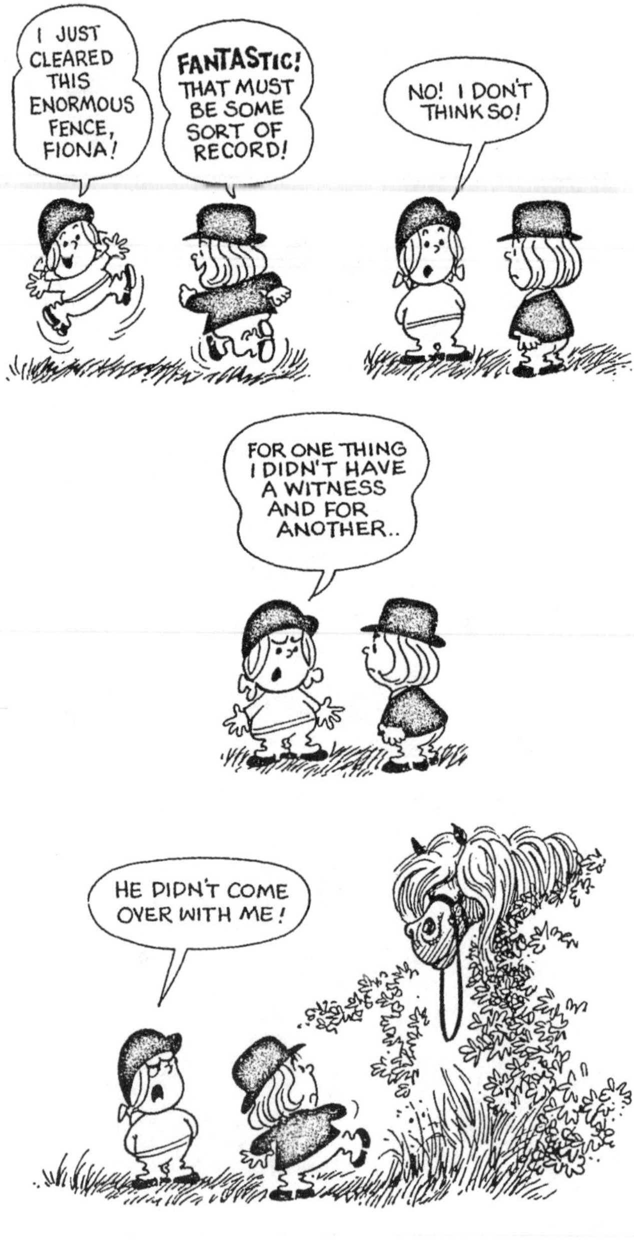
I JUST CLEARED THIS ENORMOUS FENCE, FIONA!
FANTASTIC! THAT MUST BE SOME SORT OF RECORD!
NO! I DON'T THINK SO!
FOR ONE THING I DIDN'T HAVE A WITNESS AND FOR ANOTHER..
HE DIDN'T COME OVER WITH ME!

PERHAPS IT WON'T HURT THIS TIME
MAY BE I'LL LAND LIGHTLY ON MY FEET!
WUMP!
I'VE JUST REALISED WHAT IT MEANS, FIONA!
REALISED WHAT WHAT MEANS?
IT IS BETTER TO TRAVEL HOPEFULLY THAN TO ARRIVE

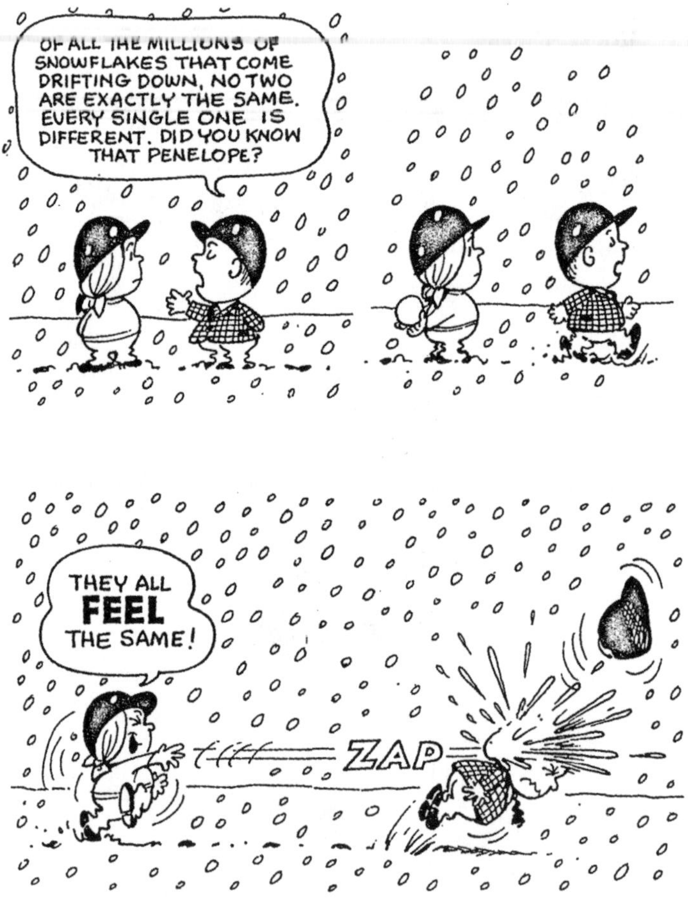
OF ALL THE MILLIONS OF SNOWFLAKES THAT COME DRIFTING DOWN, NO TWO ARE EXACTLY THE SAME. EVERY SINGLE ONE IS DIFFERENT. DID YOU KNOW THAT PENELOPE?
THEY ALL FEEL THE SAME!
ZAP

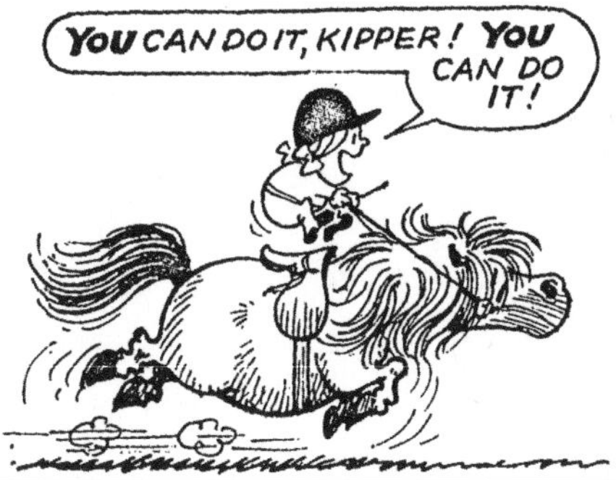
YOU CAN DO IT, KIPPER! YOU CAN DO IT!

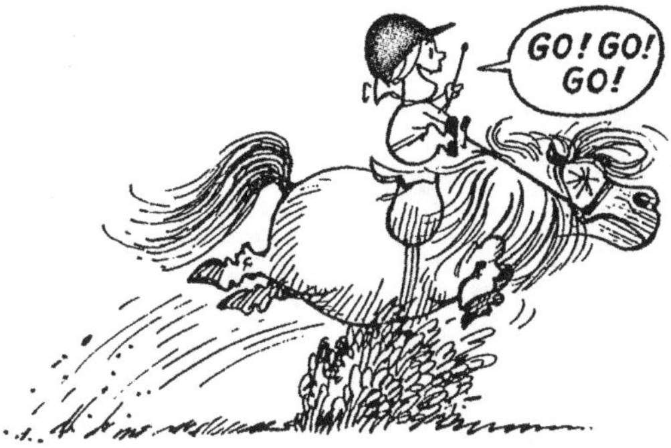
GO! GO! GO!

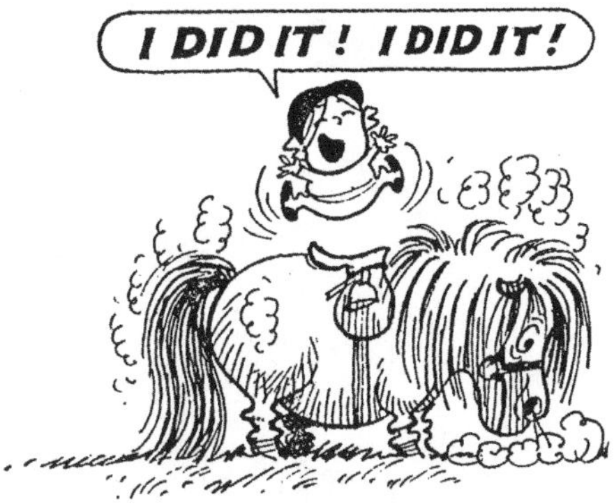
I DID IT! I DID IT!

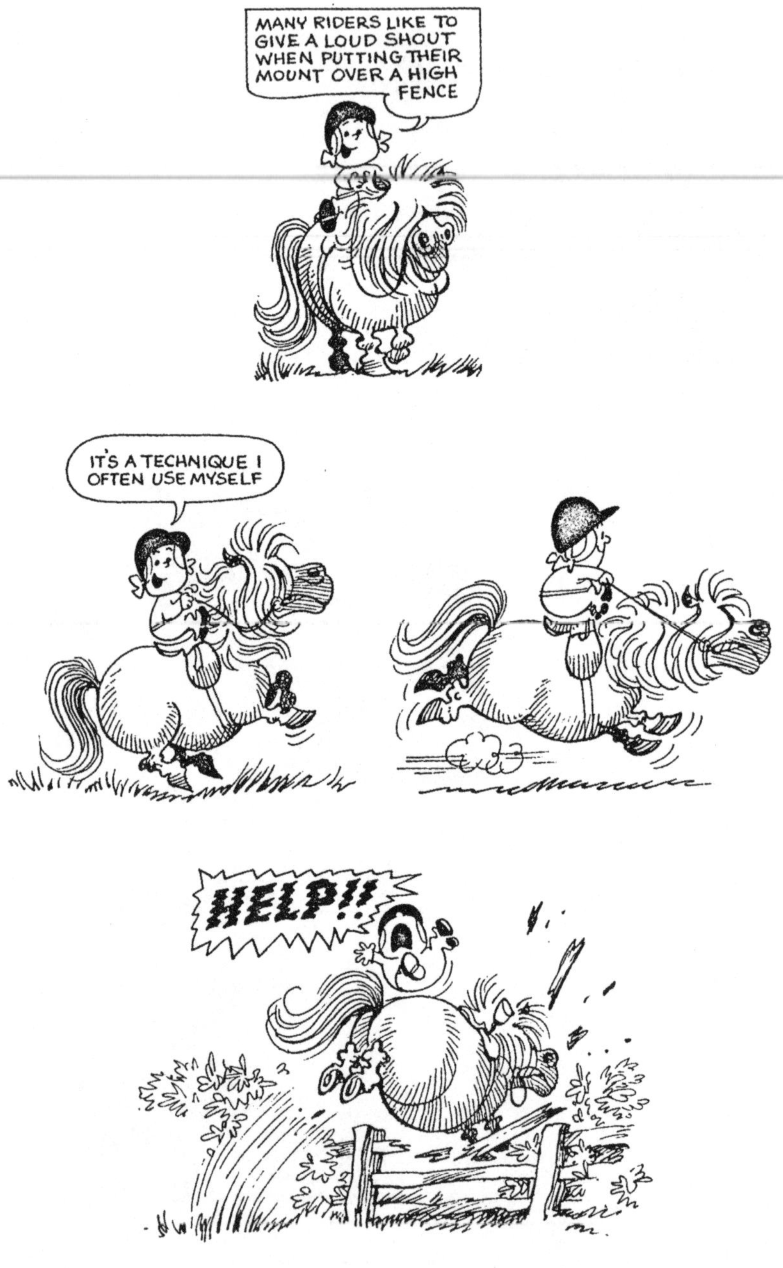
MANY RIDERS LIKE TO GIVE A LOUD SHOUT WHEN PUTTING THEIR MOUNT OVER A HIGH FENCE
IT'S A TECHNIQUE I OFTEN USE MYSELF
HELP!!

CONSIDERING HOW LITTLE WORK PUFF! THE AVERAGE PONY DOES GASP!
I USED TO WONDER PUFF! WHY THEY WERE CALLED GASP!
BEASTS OF BURDEN PHEW!
NOW I KNOW!

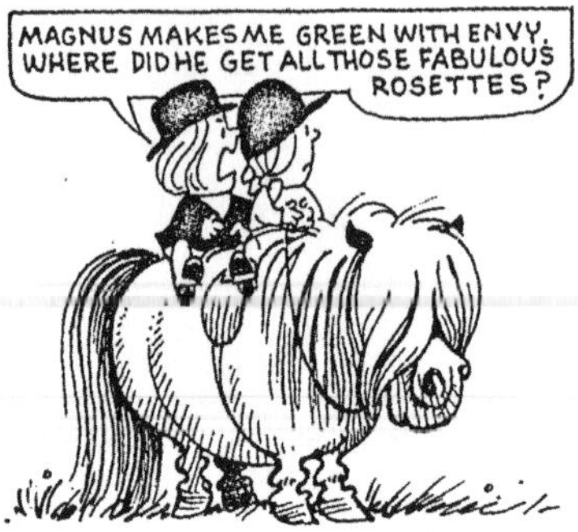
MAGNUS MAKES ME GREEN WITH ENVY, WHERE DID HE GET ALL THOSE FABULOUS ROSETTES?

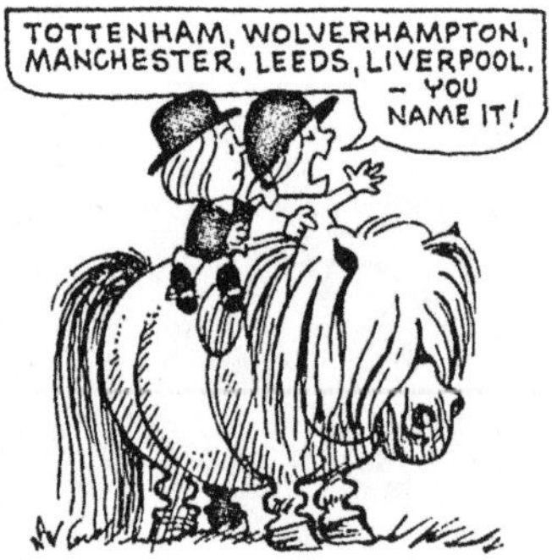
TOTTENHAM, WOLVERHAMPTON, MANCHESTER, LEEDS, LIVERPOOL. - YOU NAME IT!

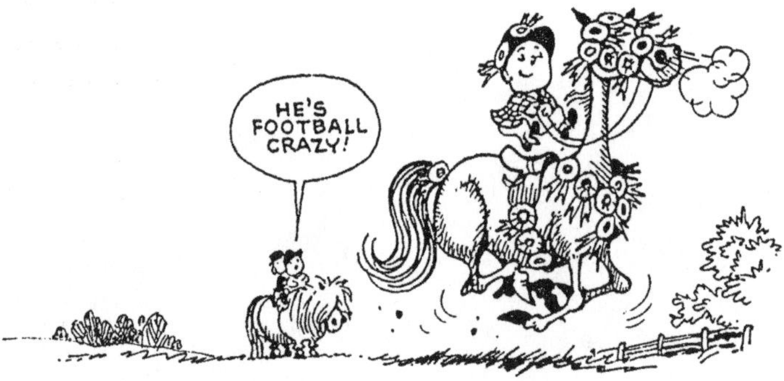
HE'S FOOTBALL CRAZY!

MAY I HAVE A RIDE PENELOPE?
NO, YOU MAY NOT! HE'S MY PONY
I DON'T KNOW WHY I'M SO UNKIND TO MY LITTLE BROTHER, TARQUIN
ALL I EVER THINK ABOUT THESE DAYS...
... IS MY OWN PLEASURE

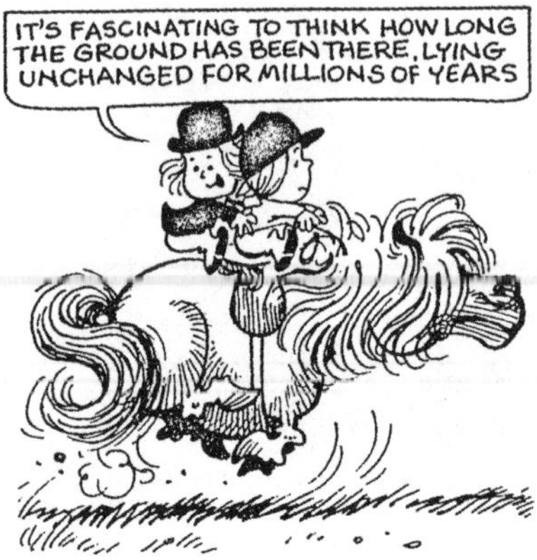
IT'S FASCINATING TO THINK HOW LONG THE GROUND HAS BEEN THERE, LYING UNCHANGED FOR MILLIONS OF YEARS

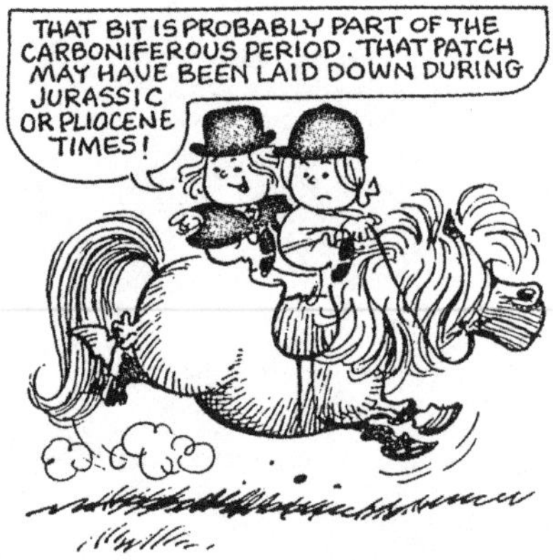
THAT BIT IS PROBABLY PART OF THE CARBONIFEROUS PERIOD. THAT PATCH MAY HAVE BEEN LAID DOWN DURING JURASSIC OR PLIOCENE TIMES!

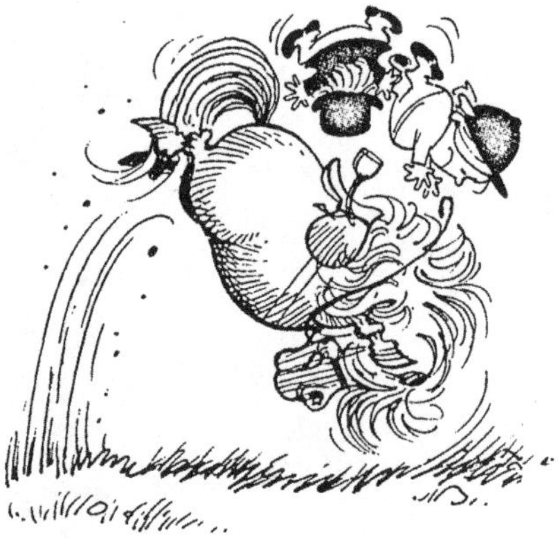

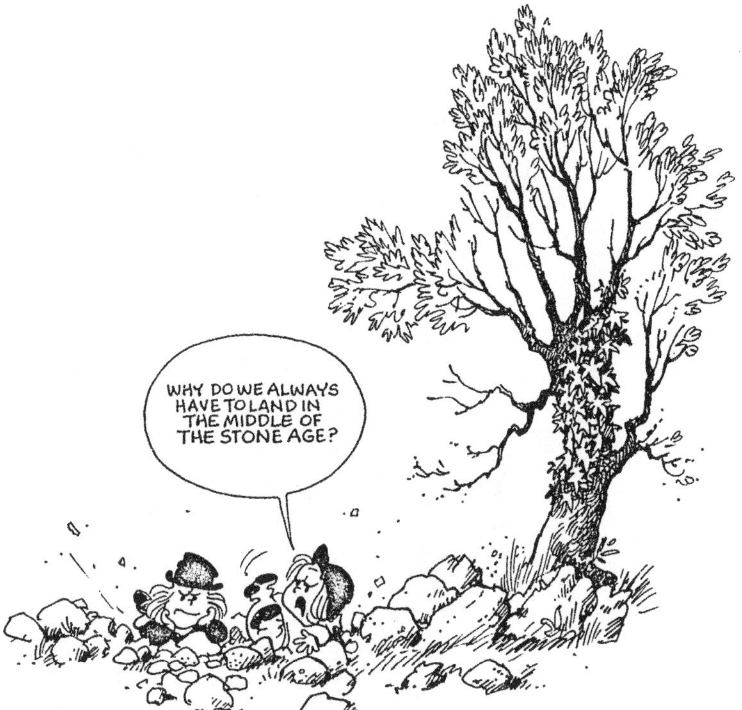
WHY DO WE ALWAYS HAVE TO LAND IN THE MIDDLE OF THE STONE AGE?

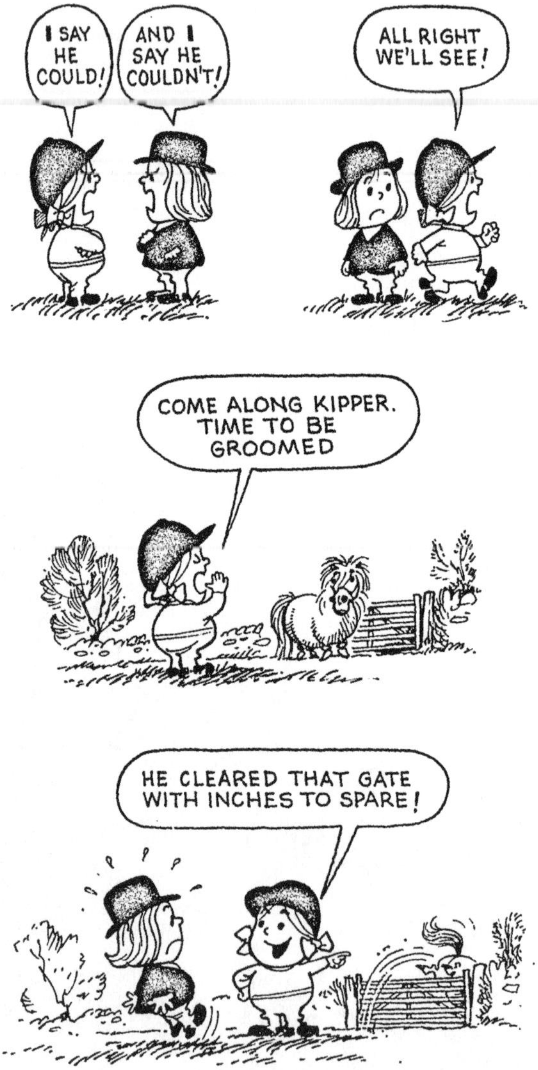
I SAY HE COULD!
AND I SAY HE COULDN'T!
ALL RIGHT WE'LL SEE!
COME ALONG KIPPER. TIME TO BE GROOMED
HE CLEARED THAT GATE WITH INCHES TO SPARE!

HERE'S SOMEONE I'M SURE YOU'D LIKE TO MEET, PENELOPE!
YOU HAVE A GREAT DEAL IN COMMON, SIMILAR INTERESTS AND PROBLEMS AND ALL THAT STUFF!
PENELOPE! MEET BILLY BOG-SPAVIN
PLEASE DON'T BOTHER TO GET UP!

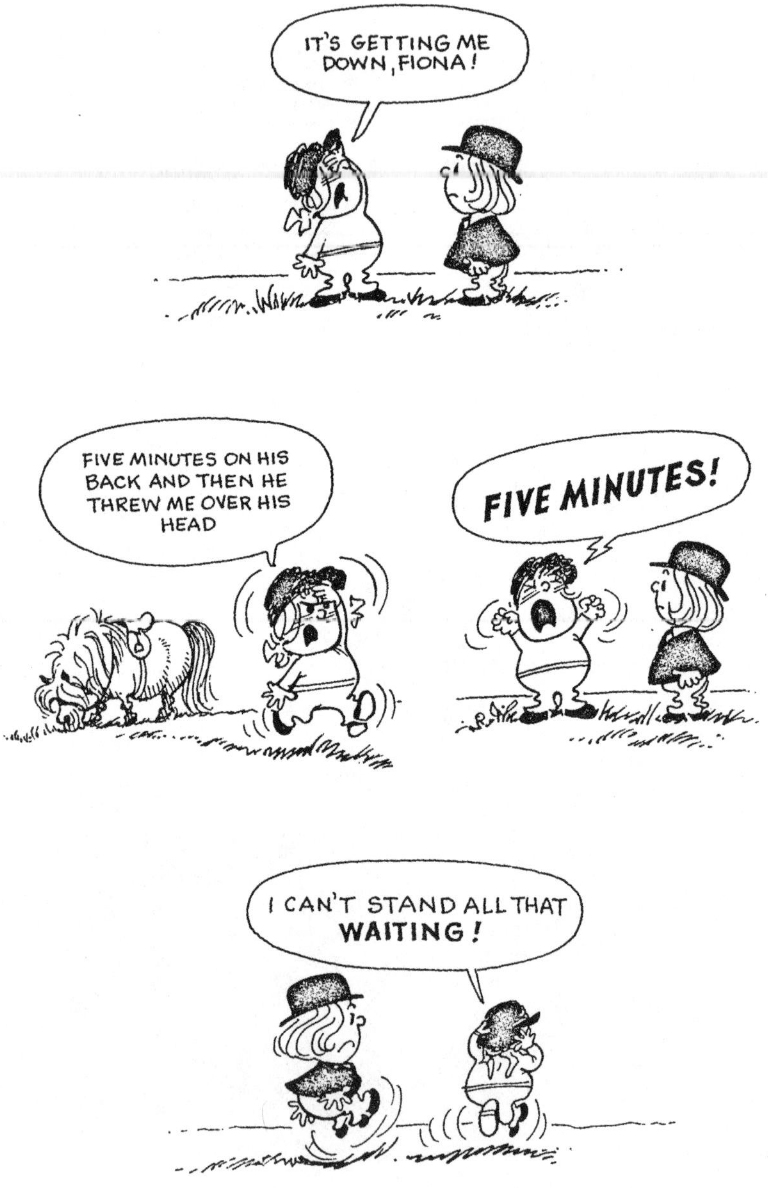
IT'S GETTING ME DOWN, FIONA!
FIVE MINUTES ON HIS BACK AND THEN HE THREW ME OVER HIS HEAD
FIVE MINUTES!
I CAN'T STAND ALL THAT WAITING!

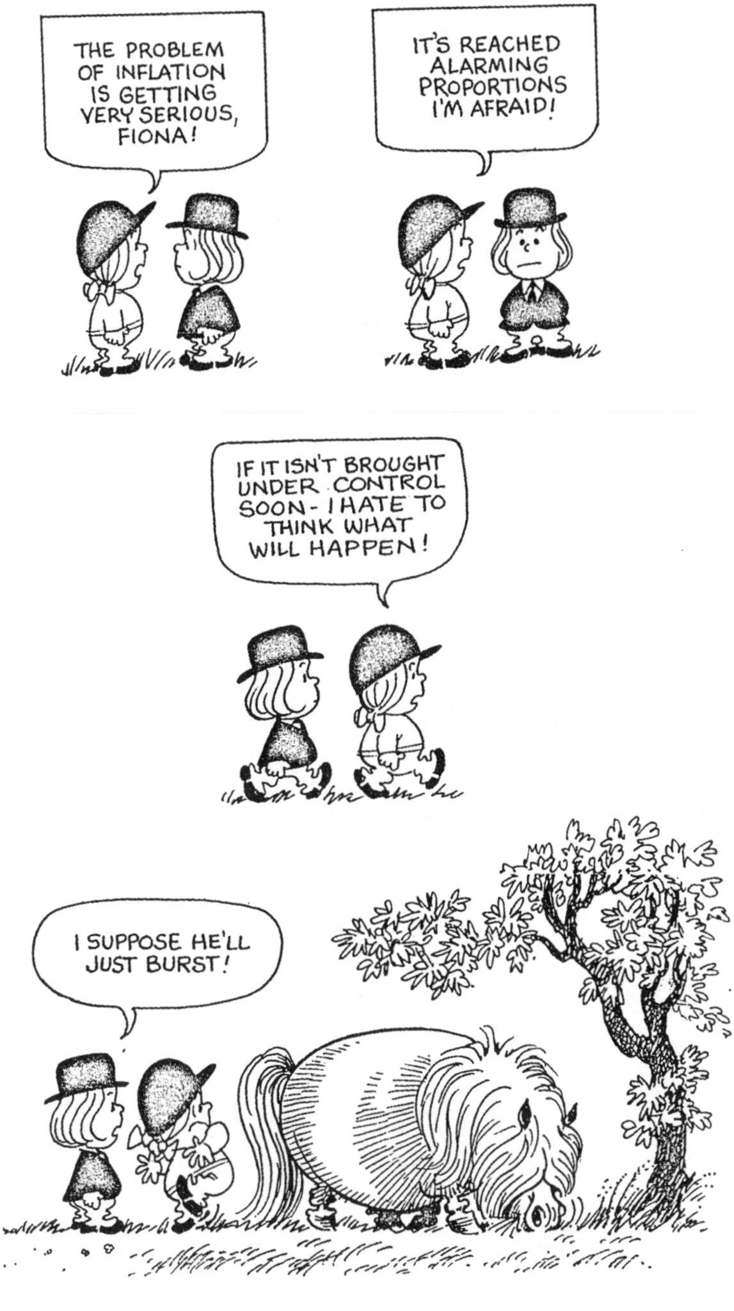
THE PROBLEM OF INFLATION IS GETTING VERY SERIOUS, FIONA!
IT'S REACHED ALARMING PROPORTIONS I'M AFRAID!
IF IT ISN'T BROUGHT UNDER CONTROL SOON - I HATE TO THINK WHAT WILL HAPPEN!
I SUPPOSE HE'LL JUST BURST!

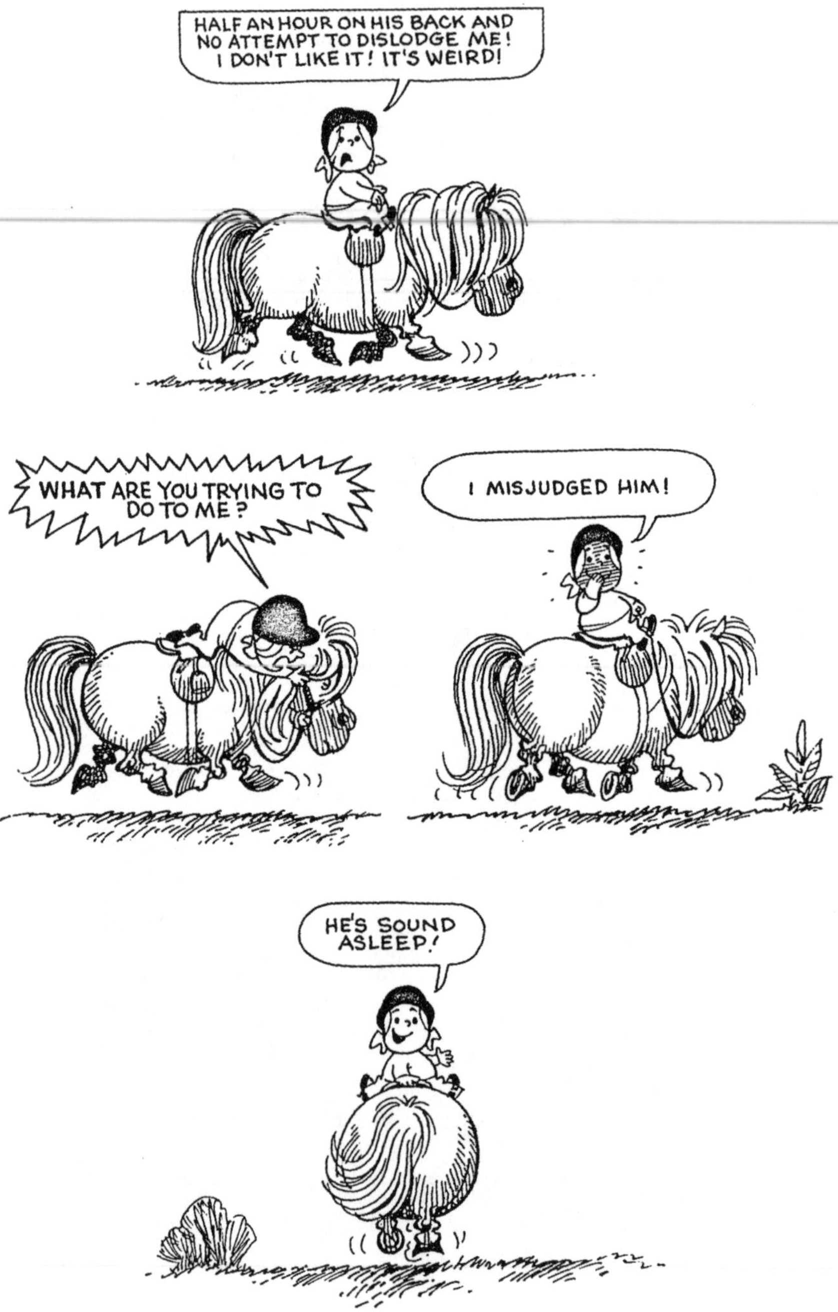
HALF AN HOUR ON HIS BACK AND NO ATTEMPT TO DISLODGE ME! I DON'T LIKE IT! IT'S WEIRD!
WHAT ARE YOU TRYING TO DO TO ME?
I MISJUDGED HIM!
HE'S SOUND ASLEEP!

FRESH AIR IS GOOD FOR YOU!
PLENTY OF PHYSICAL EXERCISE IS ESSENTAL FOR PERFECT HEALTH!
PEOPLE PAY LOTS OF MONEY FOR THE BENEFITS OF A MUD BATH ...
SO WHY DO I FEEL SO AWFUL?

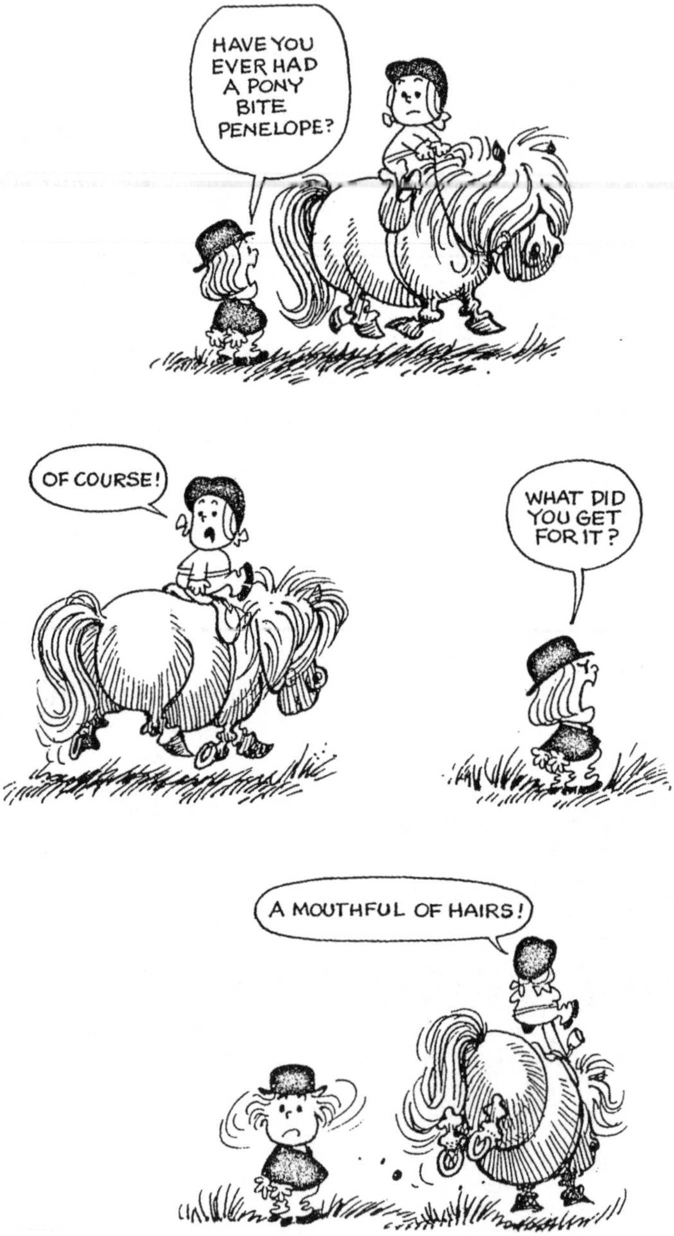
HAVE YOU EVER HAD A PONY BITE PENELOPE?
OF COURSE!
WHAT DID YOU GET FOR IT?
A MOUTHFUL OF HAIRS!

COME QUICKLY! KIPPER'S GOT COLIC. HE'S LYING ON HIS BACK WITH HIS FEET IN THE AIR
DON'T PANIC! DON'T PANIC!
IT'S JUST A DEFENCE MECHANISM
IT STOPS ANYBODY GETTING A SADDLE ON HIM WHILE HE'S ASLEEP
ZZZ

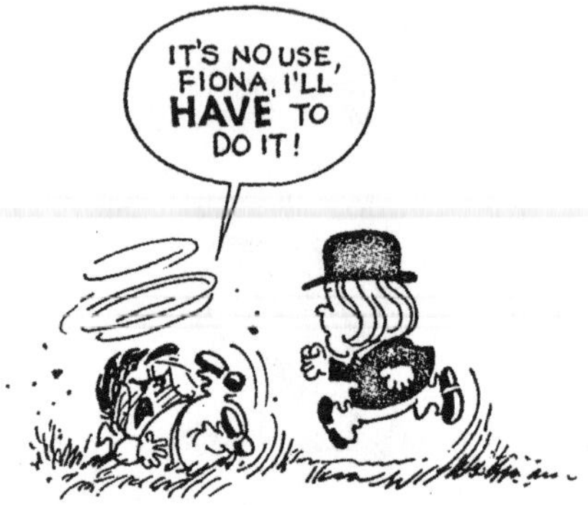
IT'S NO USE, FIONA, I'LL **HAVE** TO DO IT!

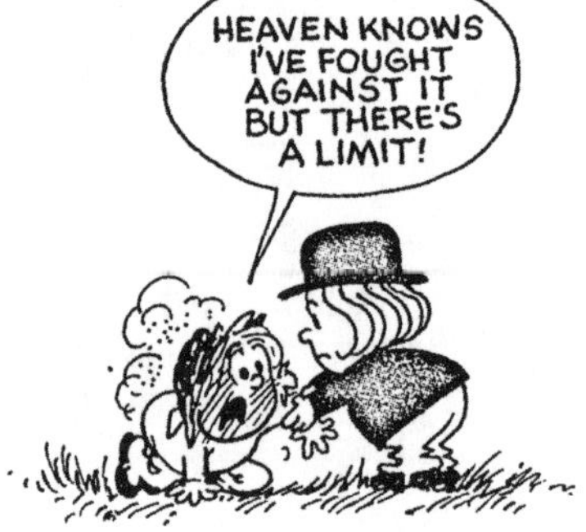
HEAVEN KNOWS I'VE FOUGHT AGAINST IT BUT THERE'S A LIMIT!

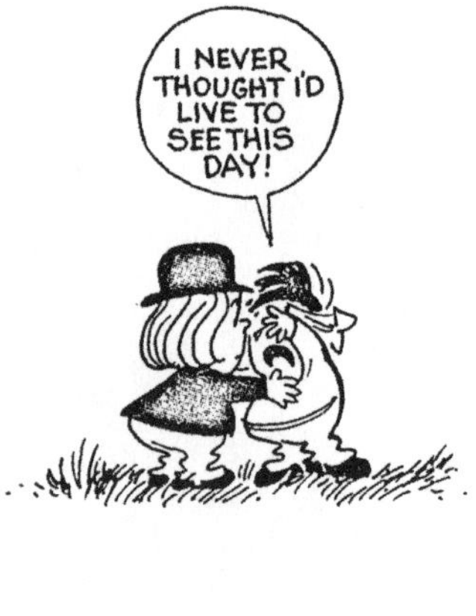
I NEVER THOUGHT I'D LIVE TO SEE THIS DAY!

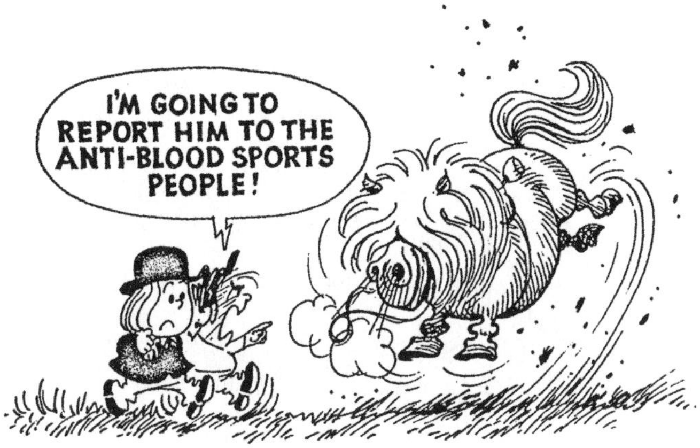
I'M GOING TO REPORT HIM TO THE ANTI-BLOOD SPORTS PEOPLE!

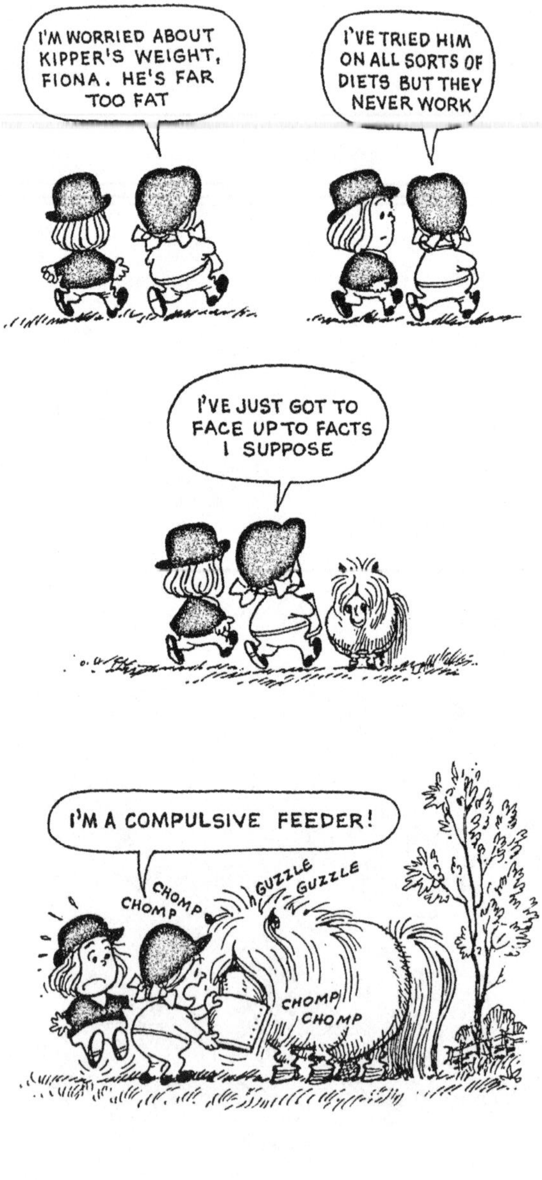
I'M WORRIED ABOUT KIPPER'S WEIGHT, FIONA. HE'S FAR TOO FAT
I'VE TRIED HIM ON ALL SORTS OF DIETS BUT THEY NEVER WORK
I'VE JUST GOT TO FACE UP TO FACTS I SUPPOSE
I'M A COMPULSIVE FEEDER!
CHOMP CHOMP
GUZZLE GUZZLE
CHOMP CHOMP

HE'S GOT A FANTASTIC MEMORY
...KNOWS EVERY FENCE AND EVERY DITCH FOR MILES...
SEE WHAT I MEAN?

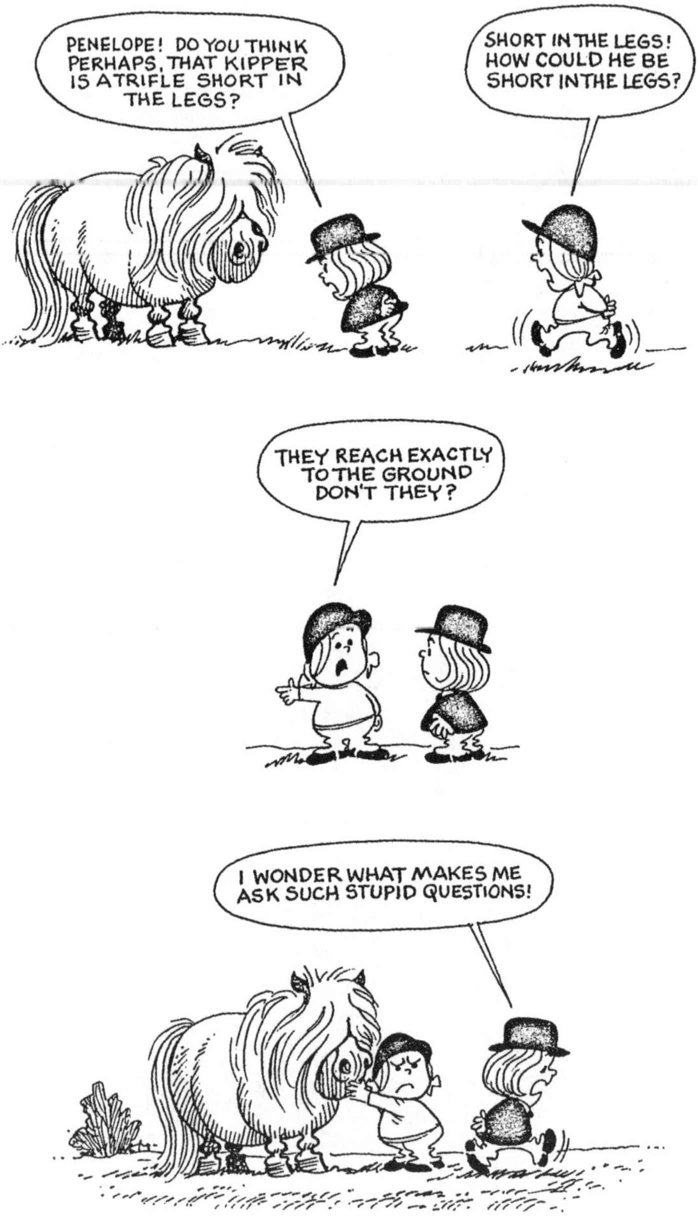
PENELOPE! DO YOU THINK PERHAPS, THAT KIPPER IS A TRIFLE SHORT IN THE LEGS?
SHORT IN THE LEGS! HOW COULD HE BE SHORT IN THE LEGS?
THEY REACH EXACTLY TO THE GROUND DON'T THEY?
I WONDER WHAT MAKES ME ASK SUCH STUPID QUESTIONS!

KIPPER'S FAR TOO FAT, FIONA!
A GOOD JOG-TROT WILL GET SOME OF HIS WEIGHT OFF!
YOU'VE LOST ABOUT FOUR POUNDS!

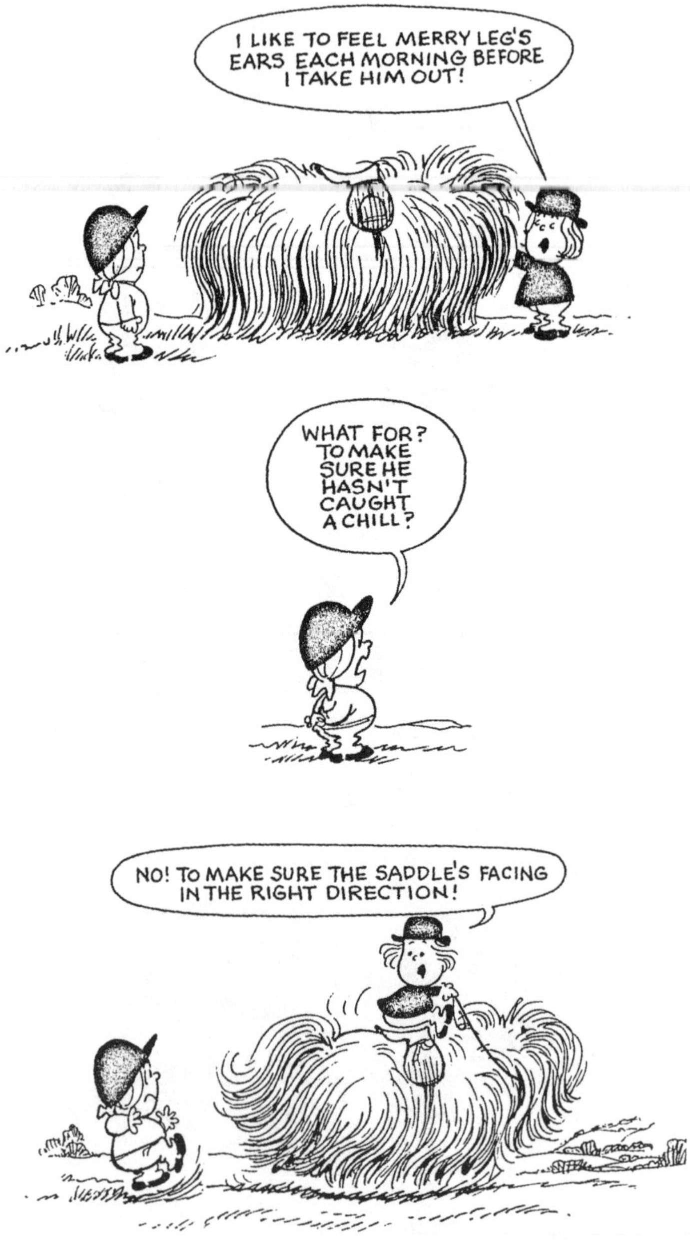
I LIKE TO FEEL MERRY LEG'S EARS EACH MORNING BEFORE I TAKE HIM OUT!
WHAT FOR? TO MAKE SURE HE HASN'T CAUGHT A CHILL?
NO! TO MAKE SURE THE SADDLE'S FACING IN THE RIGHT DIRECTION!

HOW TALL IS BILLY BOG-SPAVIN, FIONA?
SHEESH! THE QUESTIONS YOU ASK, PENELOPE!
YOU'VE SEEN HIM DOZENS OF TIMES!
I KNOW! I KNOW!
BUT I'VE NEVER SEEN HIM STANDING UP!

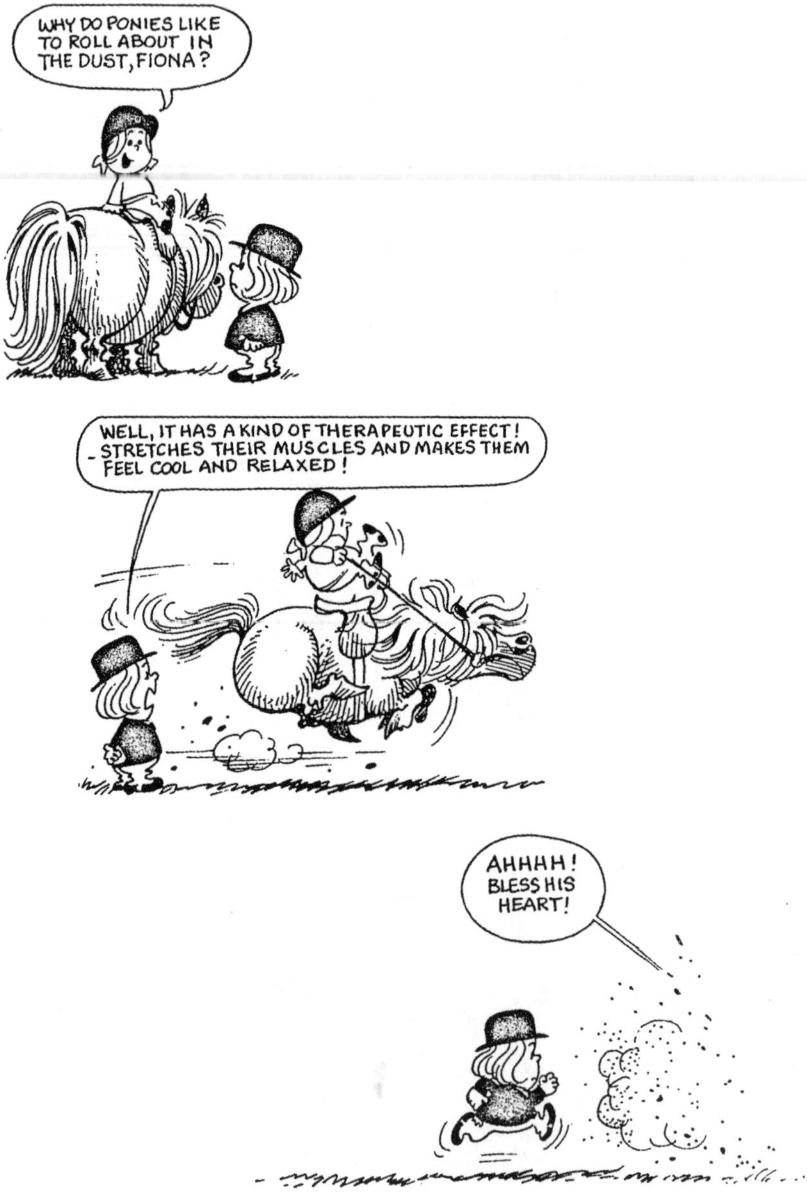
WHY DO PONIES LIKE TO ROLL ABOUT IN THE DUST, FIONA?
WELL, IT HAS A KIND OF THERAPEUTIC EFFECT! - STRETCHES THEIR MUSCLES AND MAKES THEM FEEL COOL AND RELAXED!
AHHHH! BLESS HIS HEART!

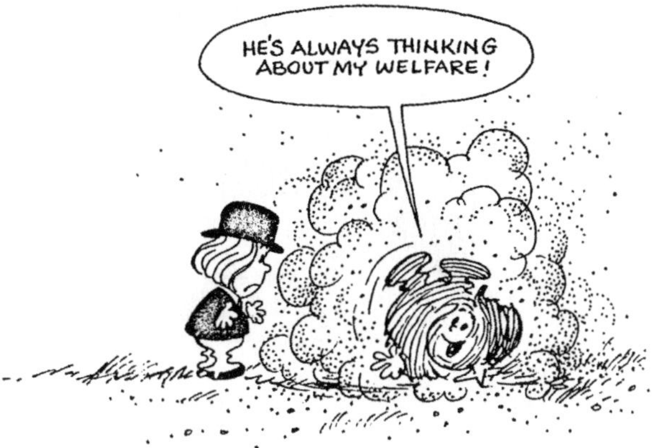
HE'S ALWAYS THINKING ABOUT MY WELFARE!

SCREAM
SCREECH
YEA YEA
BABY
SQUEEL
HOWL
YEA YEA
BABY
CRUNCH!
YOU NEVER DID LIKE MY TRANSISTOR RADIO, DID YOU ?

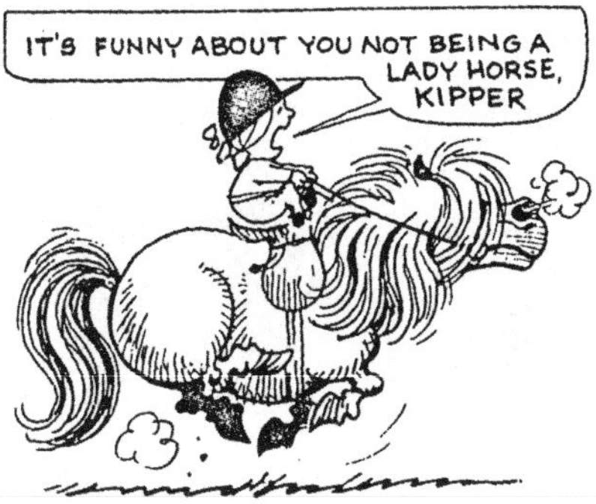
IT'S FUNNY ABOUT YOU NOT BEING A LADY HORSE, KIPPER

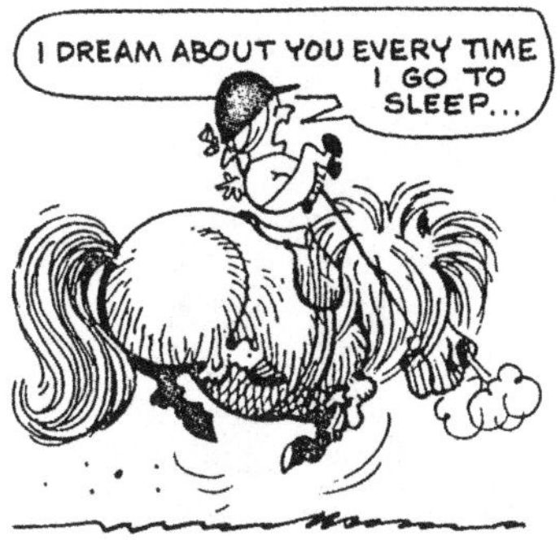
I DREAM ABOUT YOU EVERY TIME I GO TO SLEEP...

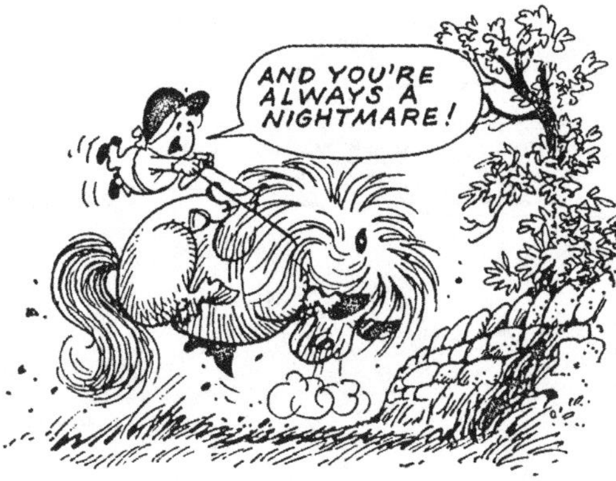
AND YOU'RE ALWAYS A NIGHTMARE!

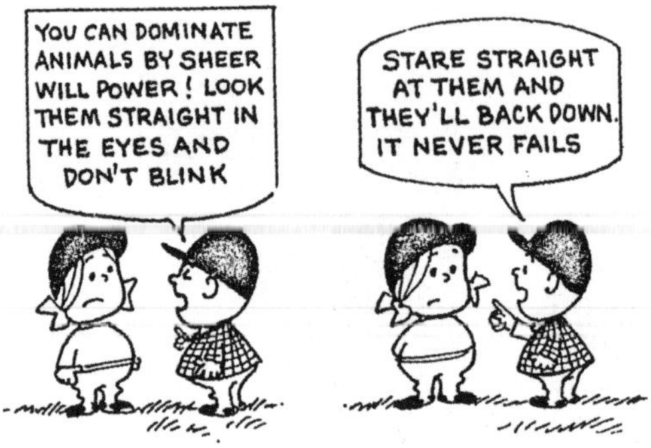
YOU CAN DOMINATE ANIMALS BY SHEER WILL POWER! LOOK THEM STRAIGHT IN THE EYES AND DON'T BLINK
STARE STRAIGHT AT THEM AND THEY'LL BACK DOWN. IT NEVER FAILS

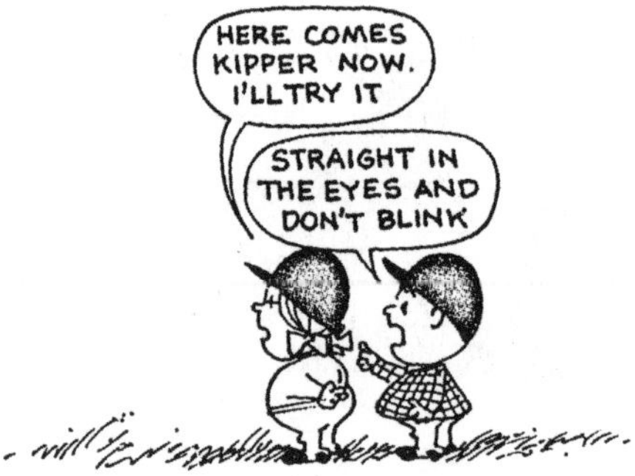
HERE COMES KIPPER NOW. I'LLTRY IT
STRAIGHT IN THE EYES AND DON'T BLINK

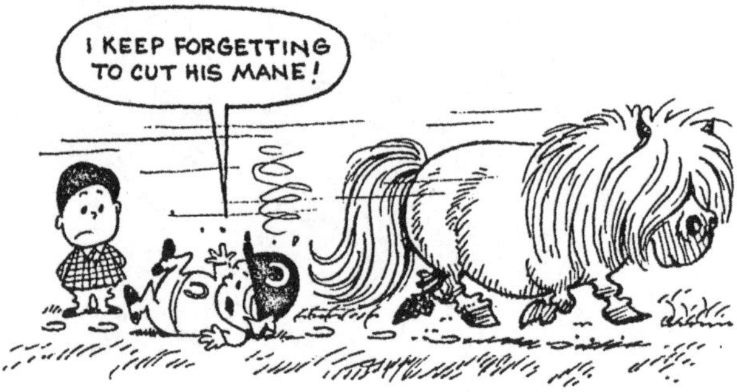
I KEEP FORGETTING TO CUT HIS MANE!

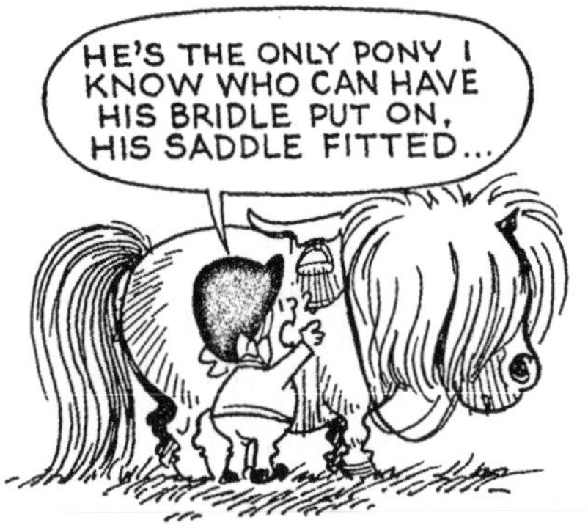
HE'S THE ONLY PONY I KNOW WHO CAN HAVE HIS BRIDLE PUT ON, HIS SADDLE FITTED...

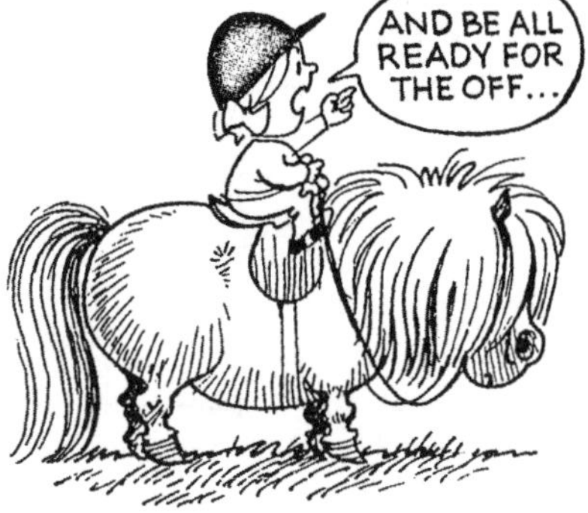
AND BE ALL READY FOR THE OFF...

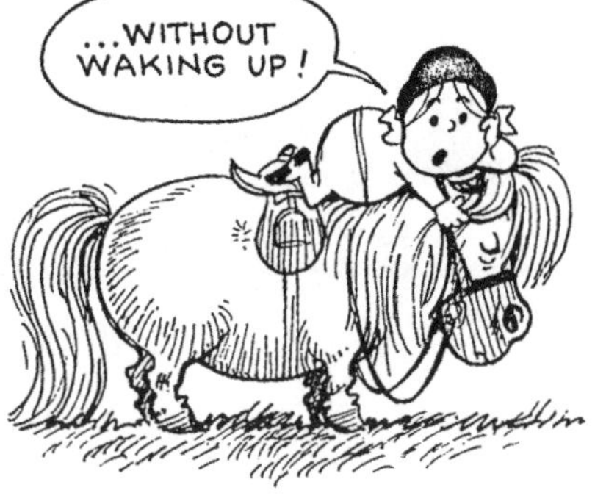
...WITHOUT WAKING UP!

RIDING IS A FASCINATING PASTIME! THERE'S SOMETHING NEW TO BE LEARNED EVERY DAY!
FOR EXAMPLE...
I'VE JUST LEARNED...
THAT SAFETY BELTS ARE A FAILURE!

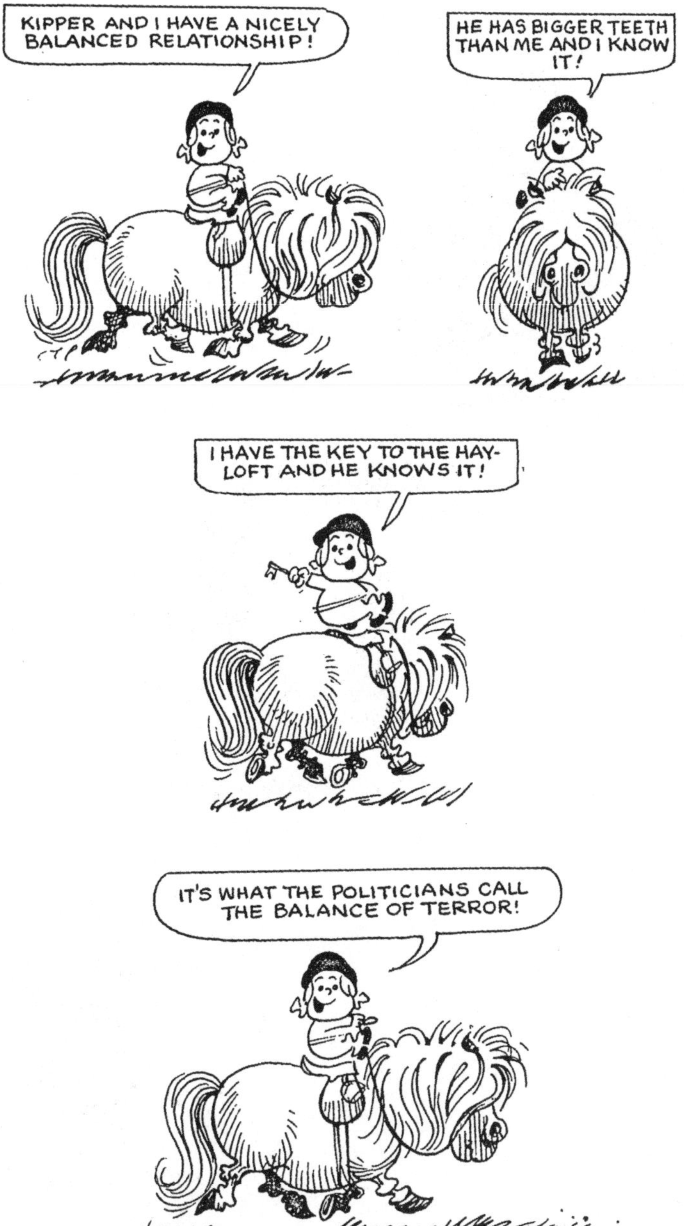
KIPPER AND I HAVE A NICELY BALANCED RELATIONSHIP!
HE HAS BIGGER TEETH THAN ME AND I KNOW IT!
I HAVE THE KEY TO THE HAY-LOFT AND HE KNOWS IT!
IT'S WHAT THE POLITICIANS CALL THE BALANCE OF TERROR!

IT'S AMAZING HOW SMOOTHLY KIPPER AND I GET ALONG TOGETHER
WE HAVE OUR UPS AND DOWNS OF COURSE!

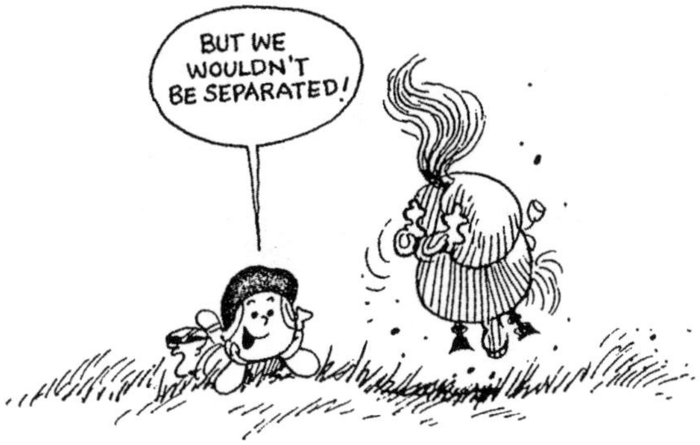
BUT WE WOULDN'T BE SEPARATED!

WELL! IF HE DOESN'T TAKE THE CAKE!
WHAT'S THE MATTER PENELOPE?
SHEESH! IF HE DOESN'T TAKE THE CAKE, I DON'T KNOW WHO DOES!
WHAT DID HE DO?
!
I KEEP TELLING YOU!
HE'S TAKEN THE CAKE!

PHOOEY! TO ALL THIS LONG GRASS!
COME ON OUT! WE KNOW YOU'RE IN THERE!
!
THAT MUST BE ABOUT AS NEAR AS YOU CAN GET TO A MARE'S NEST!

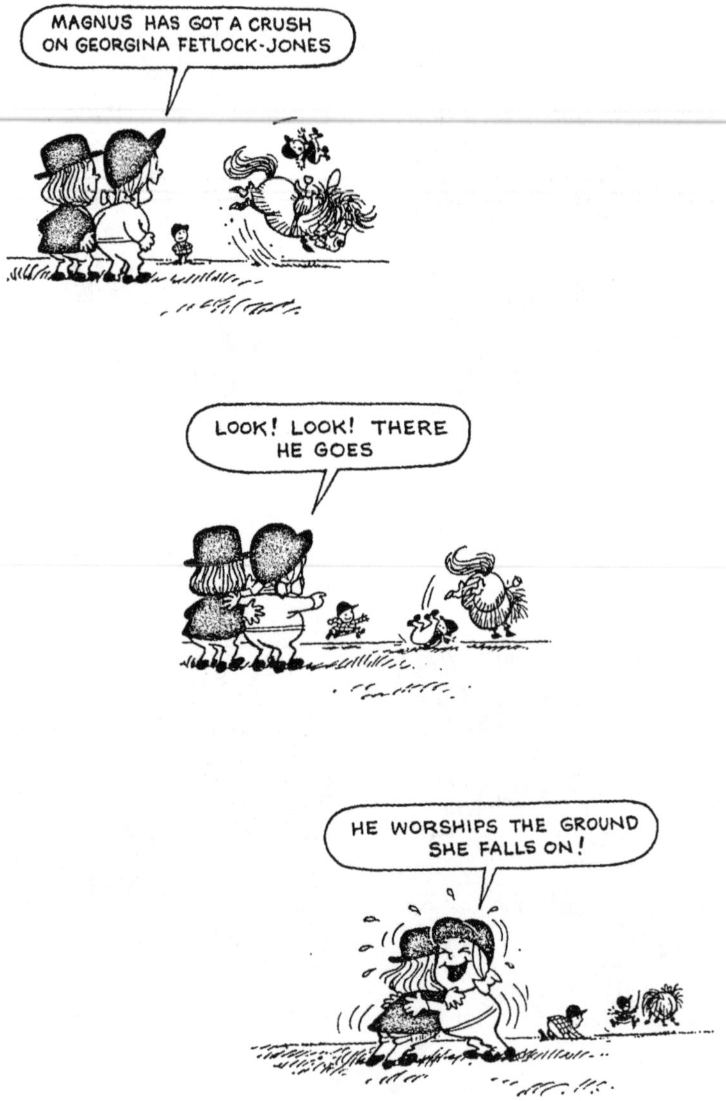
MAGNUS HAS GOT A CRUSH ON GEORGINA FETLOCK-JONES
LOOK! LOOK! THERE HE GOES
HE WORSHIPS THE GROUND SHE FALLS ON!

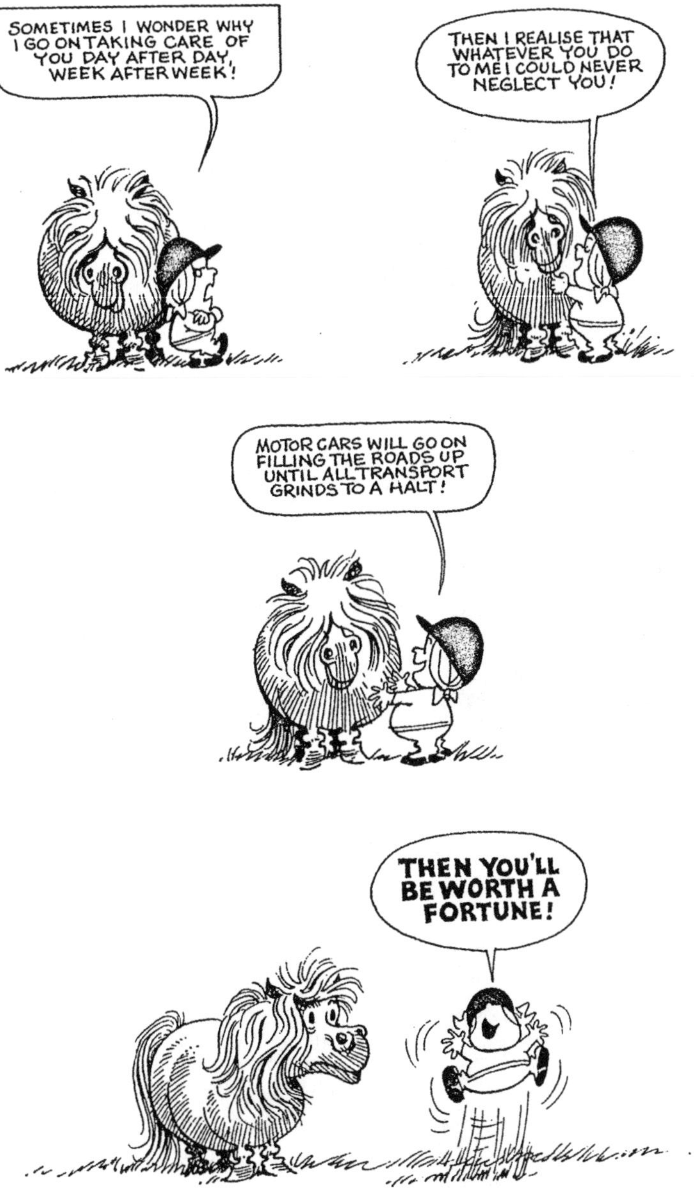
SOMETIMES I WONDER WHY I GO ON TAKING CARE OF YOU DAY AFTER DAY, WEEK AFTER WEEK!
THEN I REALISE THAT WHATEVER YOU DO TO ME I COULD NEVER NEGLECT YOU!
MOTOR CARS WILL GO ON FILLING THE ROADS UP UNTIL ALL TRANSPORT GRINDS TO A HALT!
THEN YOU'LL BE WORTH A FORTUNE!

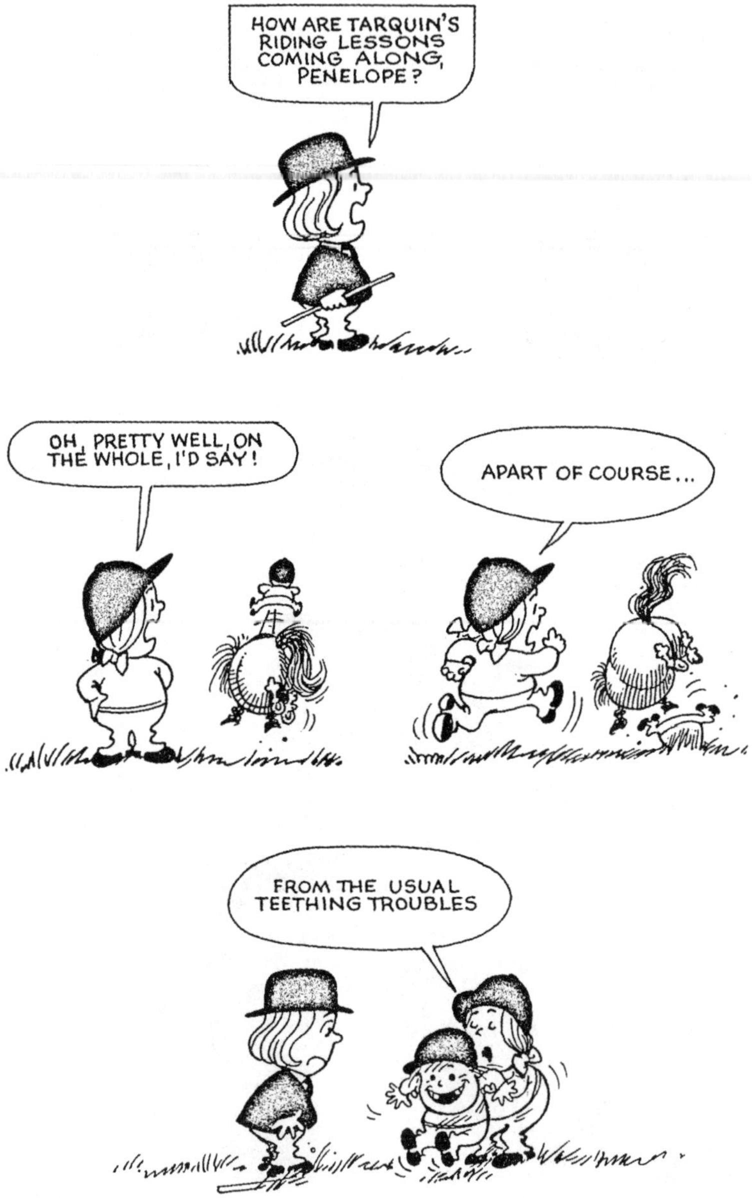
HOW ARE TARQUIN'S RIDING LESSONS COMING ALONG, PENELOPE?
OH, PRETTY WELL, ON THE WHOLE, I'D SAY!
APART OF COURSE...
FROM THE USUAL TEETHING TROUBLES

WHY ARE HORSE SHOES CONSIDERED TO BE SYMBOLS OF GOOD LUCK, PENELOPE?
I SHOULD HAVE THOUGHT THAT WAS OBVIOUS!
BEFORE THEY WERE INVENTED..
CLATTER
CLATTER
CLATTER
..YOU COULDN'T HEAR HORSES COMING!

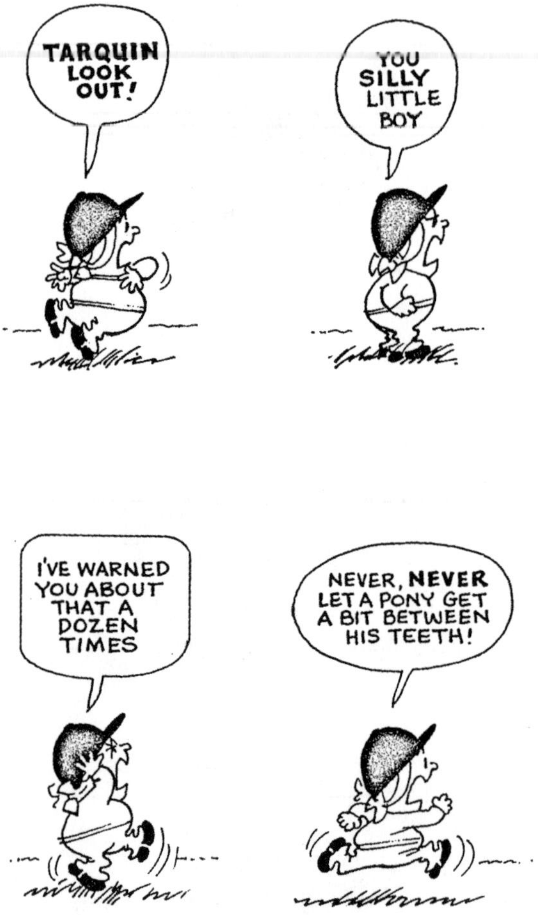
TARQUIN LOOK OUT!
YOU SILLY LITTLE BOY
I'VE WARNED YOU ABOUT THAT A DOZEN TIMES
NEVER, NEVER LET A PONY GET A BIT BETWEEN HIS TEETH!

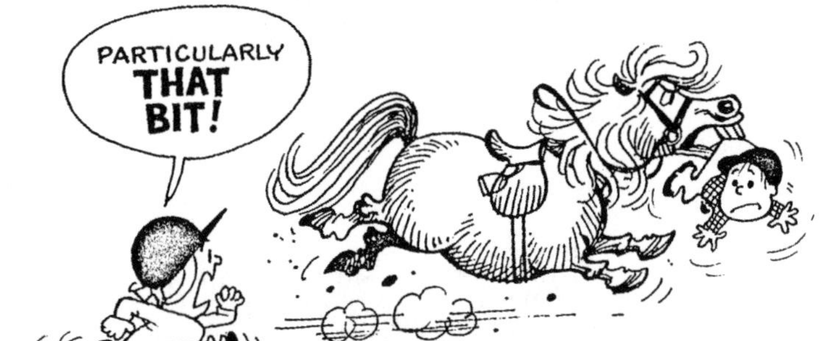
PARTICULARLY
THAT
BIT!

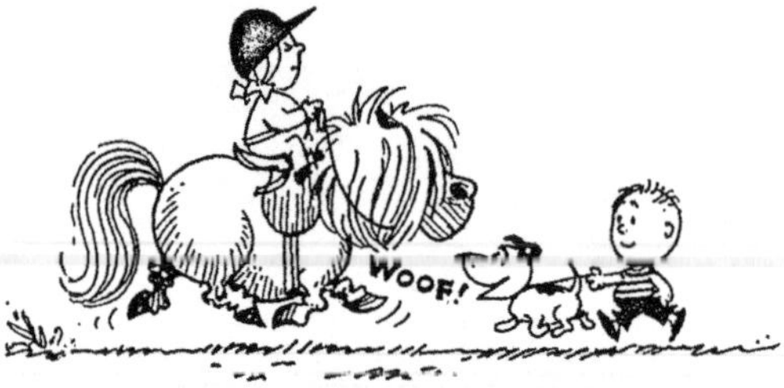
WOOF!

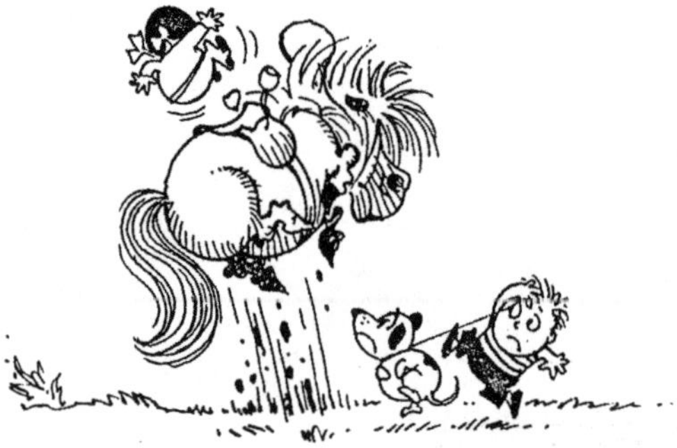

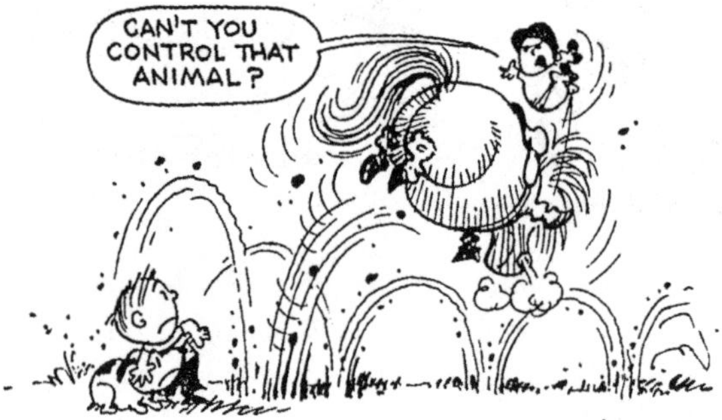
CAN'T YOU CONTROL THAT ANIMAL?

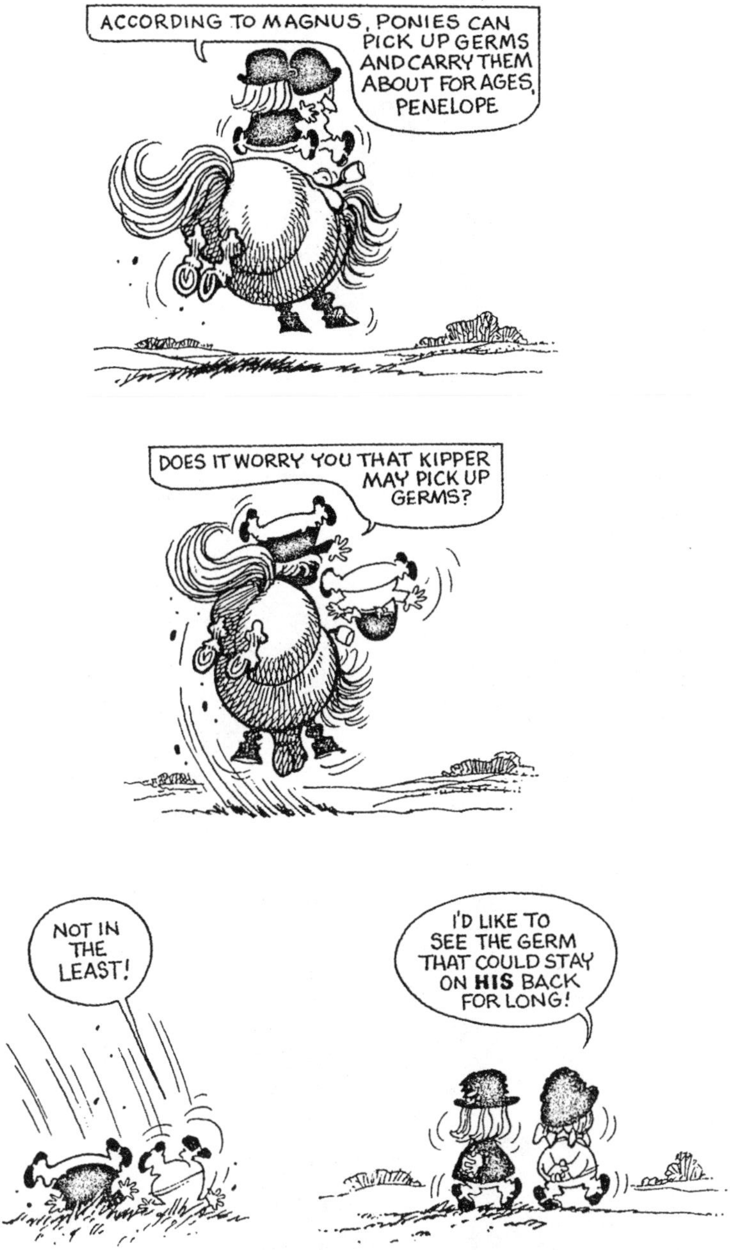
ACCORDING TO MAGNUS, PONIES CAN PICK UP GERMS AND CARRY THEM ABOUT FOR AGES, PENELOPE
DOES IT WORRY YOU THAT KIPPER MAY PICK UP GERMS?
NOT IN THE LEAST!
I'D LIKE TO SEE THE GERM THAT COULD STAY ON **HIS** BACK FOR LONG!

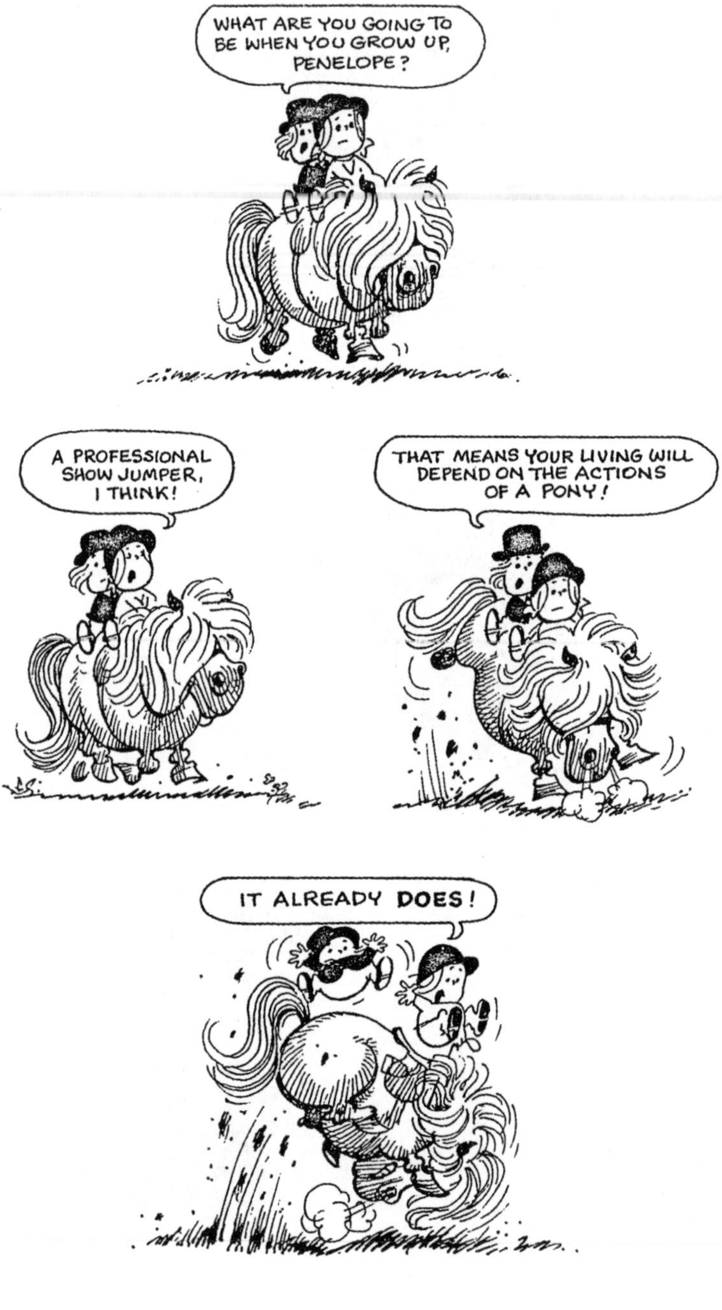
WHAT ARE YOU GOING TO BE WHEN YOU GROW UP, PENELOPE?
A PROFESSIONAL SHOW JUMPER, I THINK!
THAT MEANS YOUR LIVING WILL DEPEND ON THE ACTIONS OF A PONY!
IT ALREADY DOES!

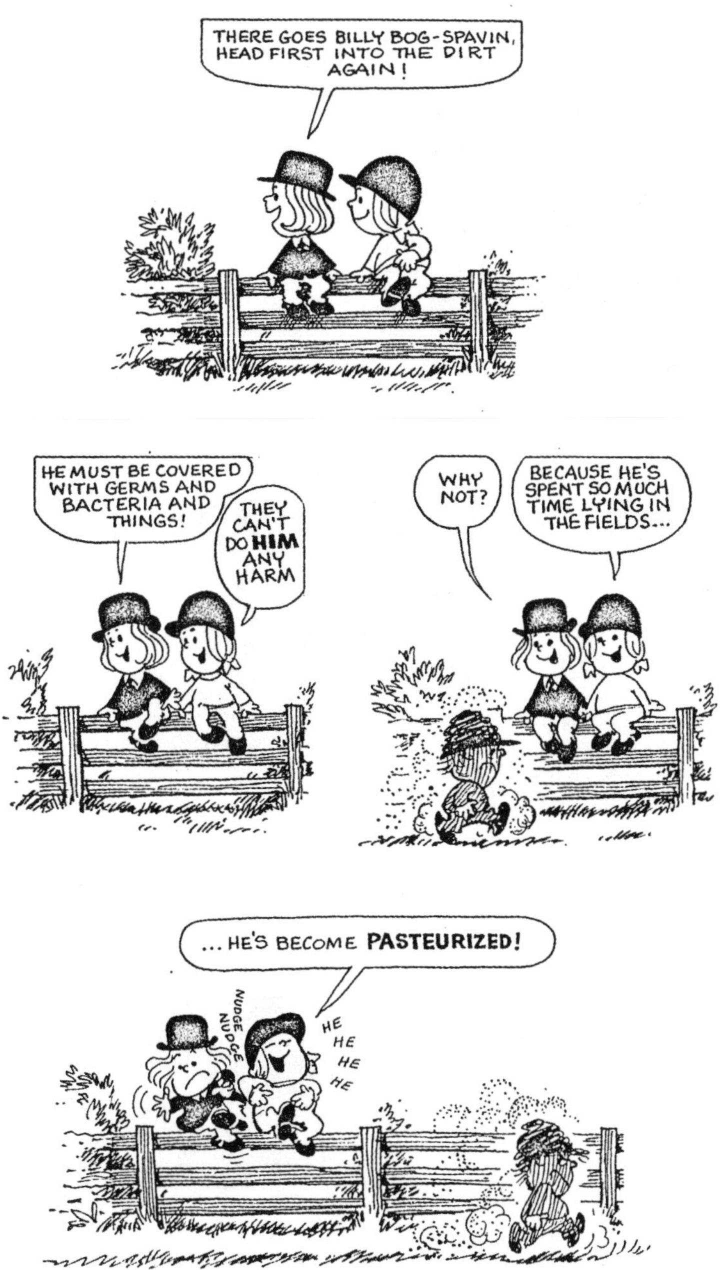
THERE GOES BILLY BOG-SPAVIN, HEAD FIRST INTO THE DIRT AGAIN!
HE MUST BE COVERED WITH GERMS AND BACTERIA AND THINGS!
THEY CAN'T DO **HIM** ANY HARM
WHY NOT?
BECAUSE HE'S SPENT SO MUCH TIME LYING IN THE FIELDS...
... HE'S BECOME **PASTEURIZED!**
NUDGE NUDGE
HE HE HE HE

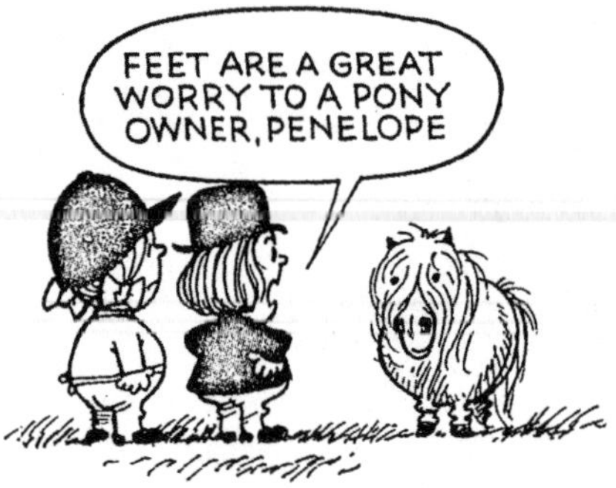
FEET ARE A GREAT WORRY TO A PONY OWNER, PENELOPE

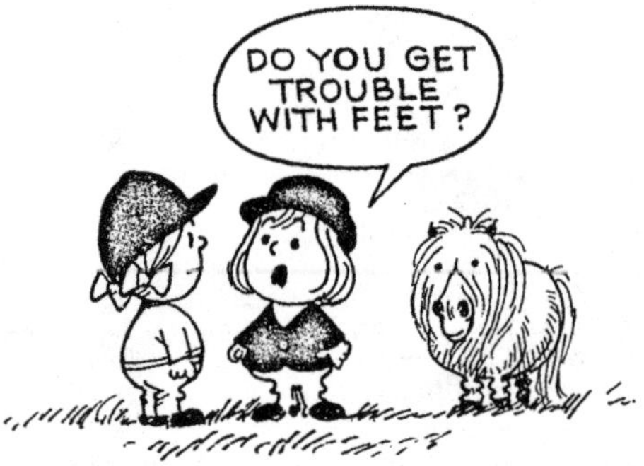
DO YOU GET TROUBLE WITH FEET ?

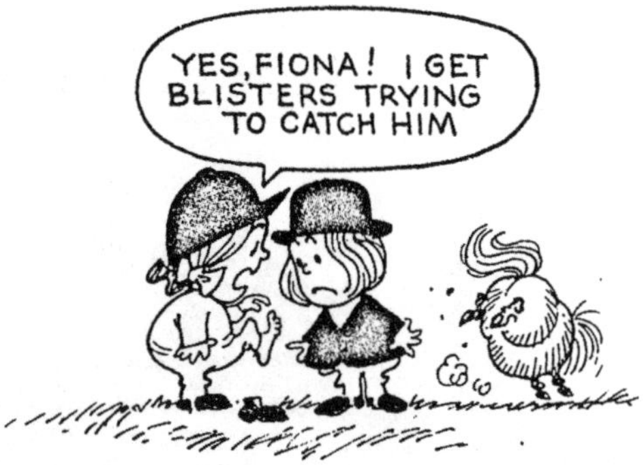
YES, FIONA! I GET BLISTERS TRYING TO CATCH HIM

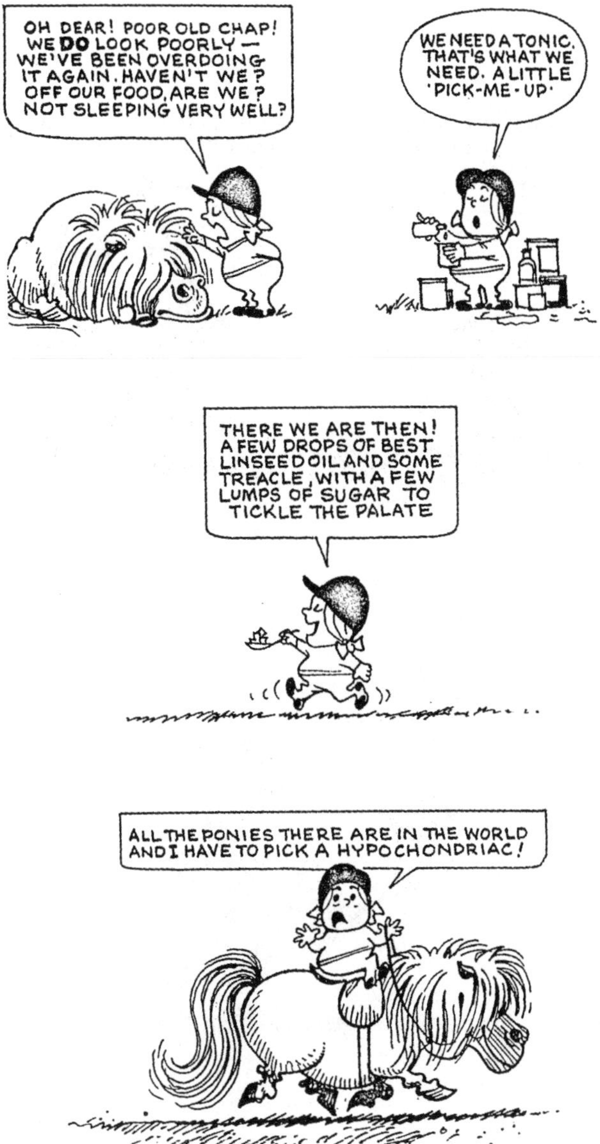
OH DEAR! POOR OLD CHAP! WE DO LOOK POORLY — WE'VE BEEN OVERDOING IT AGAIN. HAVEN'T WE? OFF OUR FOOD, ARE WE? NOT SLEEPING VERY WELL?
WE NEED A TONIC. THAT'S WHAT WE NEED. A LITTLE 'PICK-ME-UP'
THERE WE ARE THEN! A FEW DROPS OF BEST LINSEED OIL AND SOME TREACLE, WITH A FEW LUMPS OF SUGAR TO TICKLE THE PALATE
ALL THE PONIES THERE ARE IN THE WORLD AND I HAVE TO PICK A HYPOCHONDRIAC!

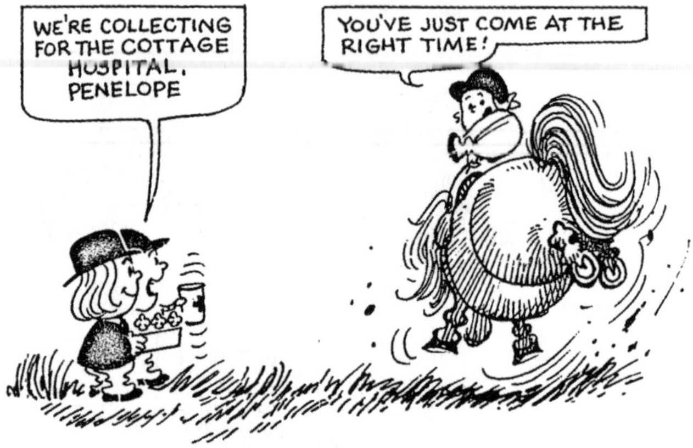
WE'RE COLLECTING FOR THE COTTAGE HOSPITAL, PENELOPE
YOU'VE JUST COME AT THE RIGHT TIME!

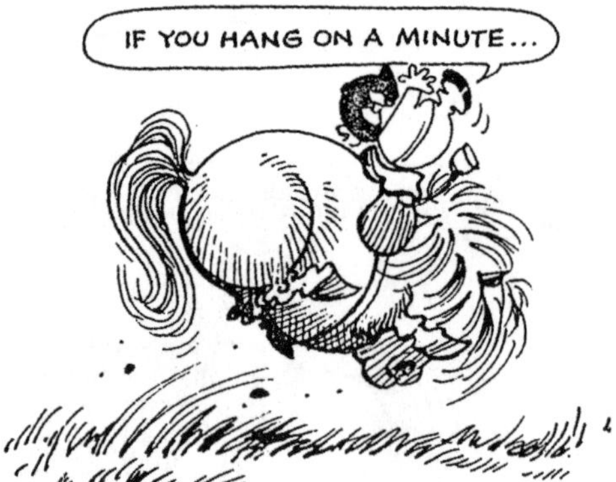
IF YOU HANG ON A MINUTE...

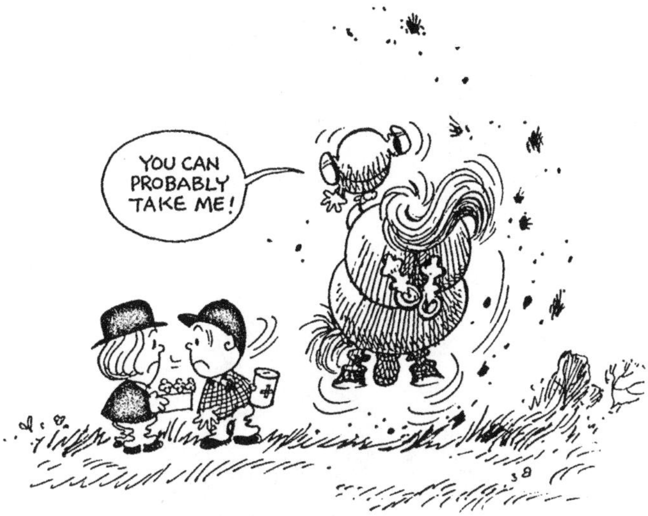
YOU CAN PROBABLY TAKE ME!

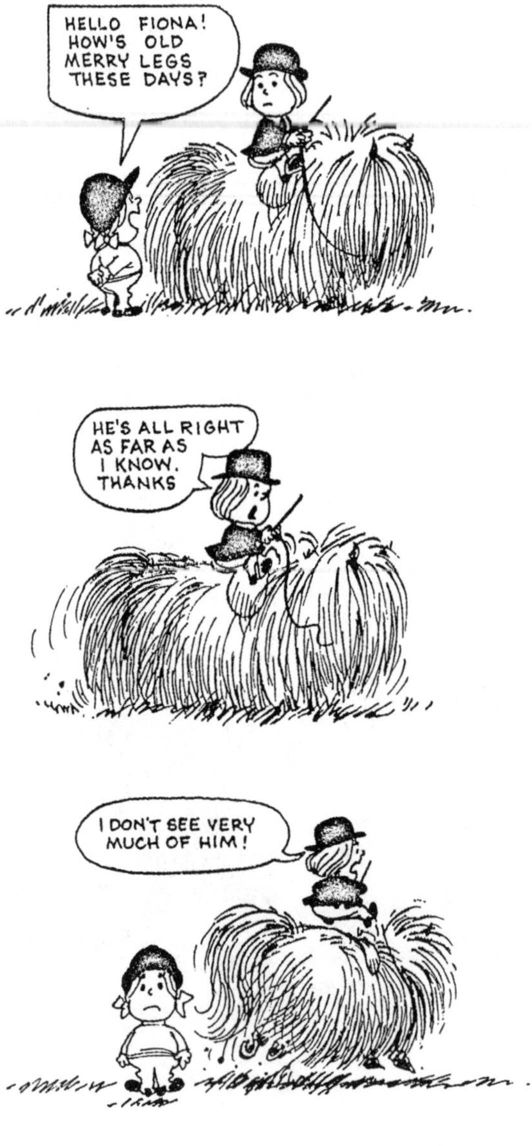
HELLO FIONA! HOW'S OLD MERRY LEGS THESE DAYS?
HE'S ALL RIGHT AS FAR AS I KNOW. THANKS
I DON'T SEE VERY MUCH OF HIM!

MY WATCH IS GUARANTEED DUSTPROOF!
WATERPROOF!
SHOCKPROOF!
IT MUST HAVE HAD A FAULTY STRAP!

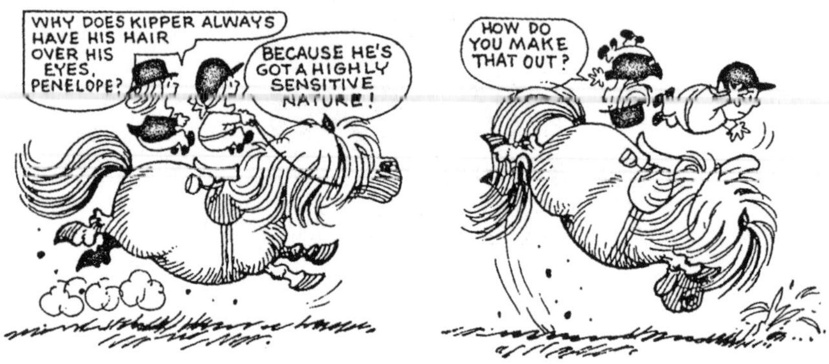
WHY DOES KIPPER ALWAYS HAVE HIS HAIR OVER HIS EYES, PENELOPE?
BECAUSE HE'S GOT A HIGHLY SENSITIVE NATURE!
HOW DO YOU MAKE THAT OUT?

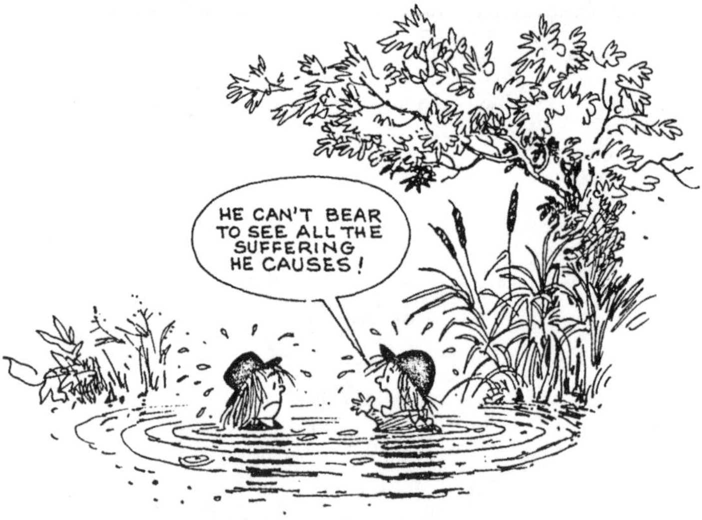
HE CAN'T BEAR TO SEE ALL THE SUFFERING HE CAUSES!

YOUR LITTLE BROTHER TARQUIN IS THE BRAVEST KID I KNOW, PENELOPE!
HE'S ALWAYS FALLING OFF HIS PONY BUT I NEVER HEAR HIM COMPLAIN
IT'S NOT THAT HE DOESN'T WANT TO...
HE NEVER HAS ENOUGH BREATH!

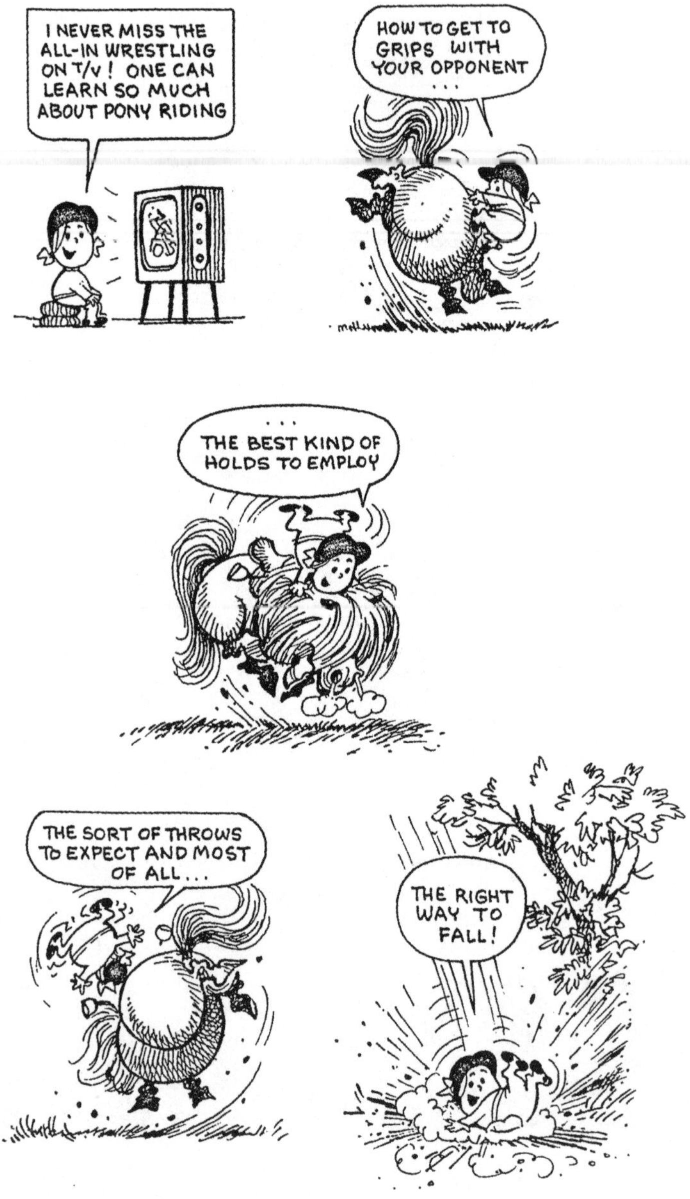
I NEVER MISS THE ALL-IN WRESTLING ON T/V! ONE CAN LEARN SO MUCH ABOUT PONY RIDING
HOW TO GET TO GRIPS WITH YOUR OPPONENT . . .
. . . THE BEST KIND OF HOLDS TO EMPLOY
THE SORT OF THROWS TO EXPECT AND MOST OF ALL . . .
THE RIGHT WAY TO FALL!

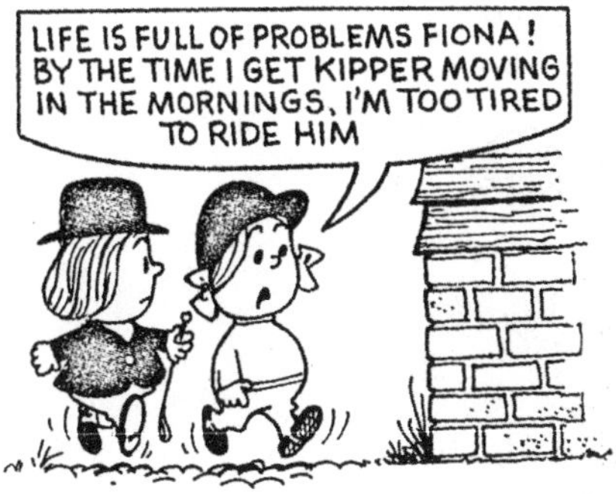
LIFE IS FULL OF PROBLEMS FIONA! BY THE TIME I GET KIPPER MOVING IN THE MORNINGS, I'M TOO TIRED TO RIDE HIM

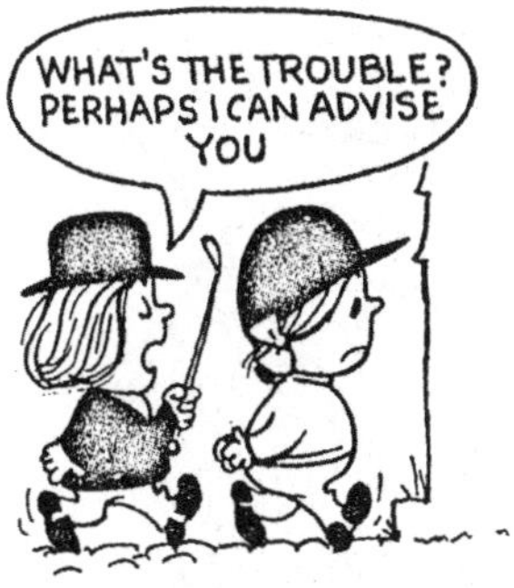
WHAT'S THE TROUBLE? PERHAPS I CAN ADVISE YOU

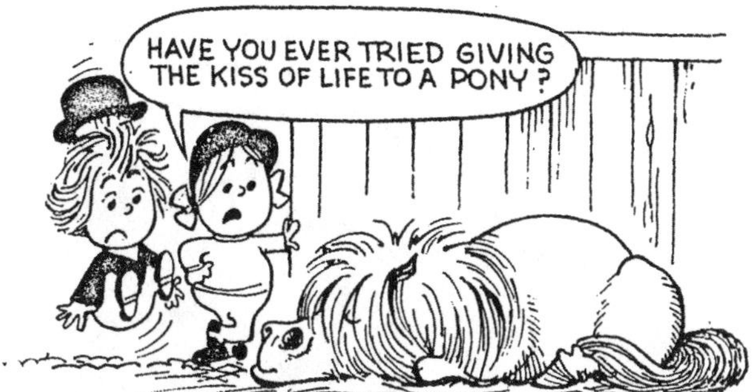
HAVE YOU EVER TRIED GIVING THE KISS OF LIFE TO A PONY?

DO YOU THINK THAT EVERYONE SHOULD BE TAUGHT ABOUT THE NEED FOR NATURE CONSERVANCY, PENELOPE?
OF COURSE I DO!
WE MUST ALL DO OUR BEST TO ENSURE THE SURVIVAL OF OUR FELLOW CREATURES FIONA!
THE TROUBLE IS....

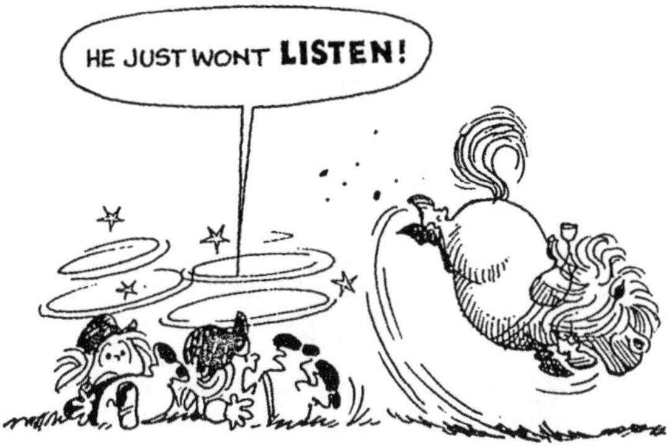
HE JUST WONT LISTEN!

HORSES NEED TO BE UNDERSTOOD, FIONA! IT'S UP TO US TO FIND OUT WHAT MOTIVATES THEIR ACTIONS, TO STUDY THEIR BEHAVIOUR PATTERNS AND TO SYMPATHISE!
WE SHOULD NEVER FAIL TO SHOW OUR SYMPATHY AND UNDERSTANDING EVEN WHEN THEY ACT LIKE BEASTS!
AFTER ALL, THEY'RE ONLY HUMAN!
I ENVY HER UNCANNY GRASP OF EQUINE PSYCHOLOGY!

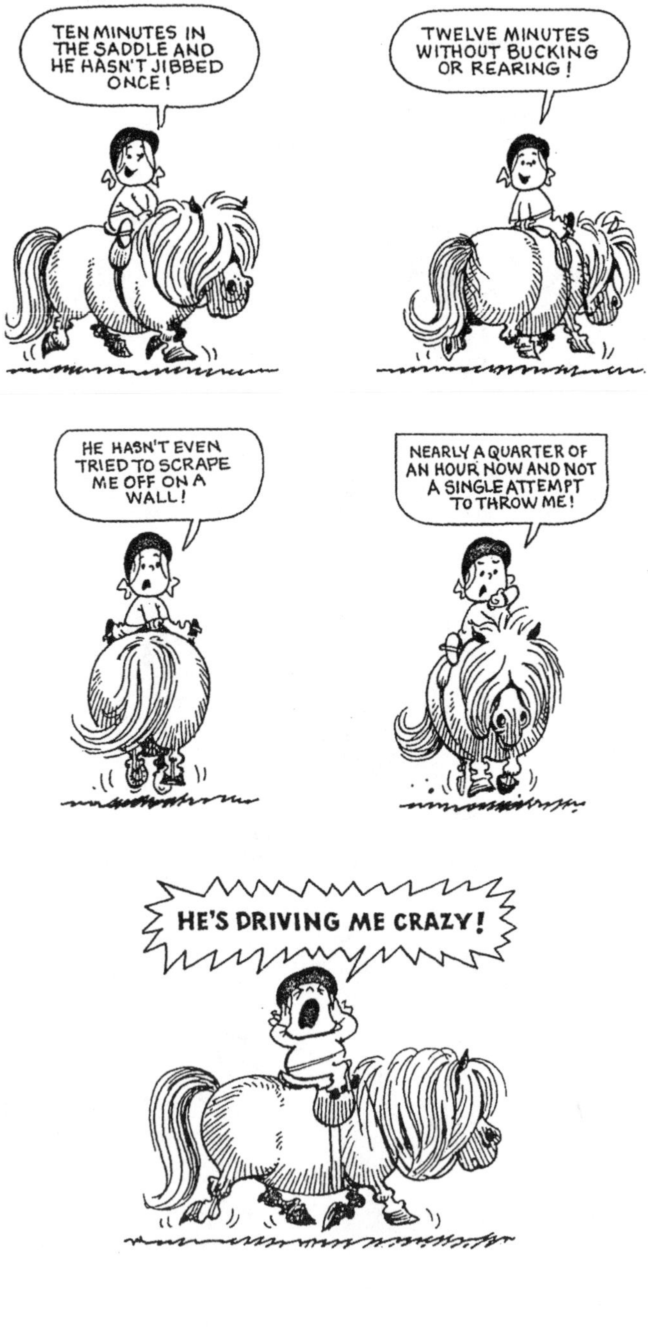
TEN MINUTES IN THE SADDLE AND HE HASN'T JIBBED ONCE!
TWELVE MINUTES WITHOUT BUCKING OR REARING!
HE HASN'T EVEN TRIED TO SCRAPE ME OFF ON A WALL!
NEARLY A QUARTER OF AN HOUR NOW AND NOT A SINGLE ATTEMPT TO THROW ME!
HE'S DRIVING ME CRAZY!

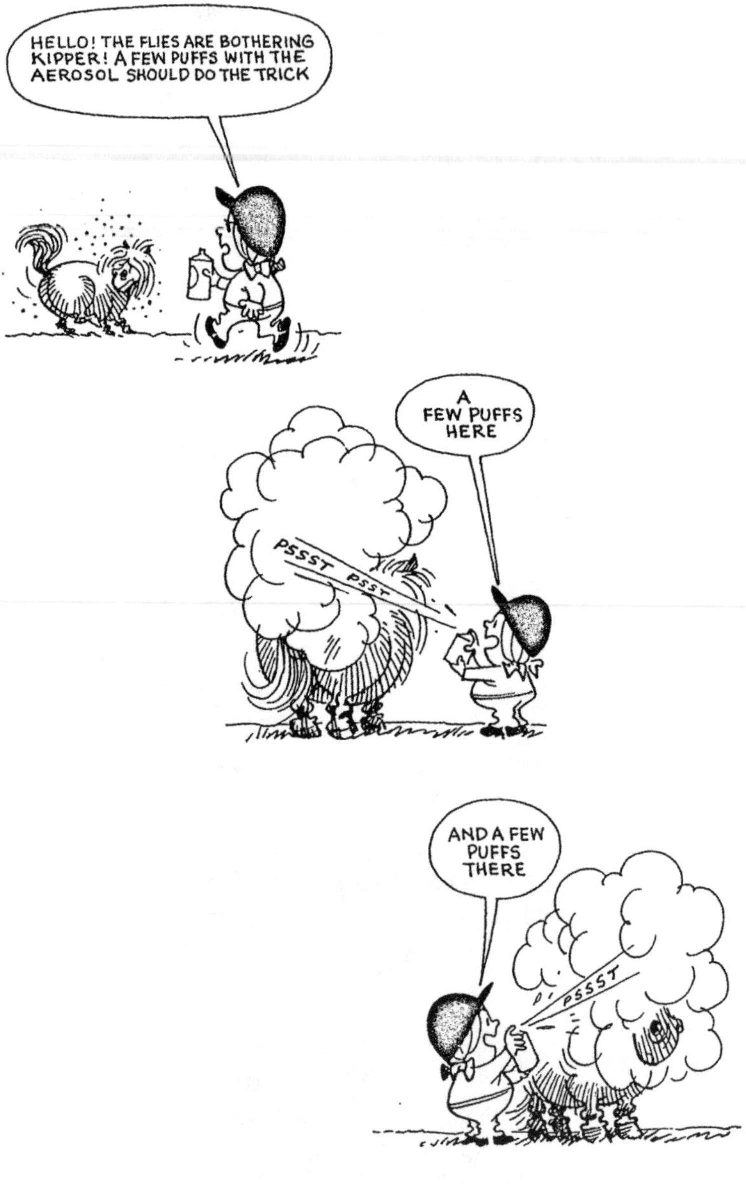
HELLO! THE FLIES ARE BOTHERING KIPPER! A FEW PUFFS WITH THE AEROSOL SHOULD DO THE TRICK
A FEW PUFFS HERE
PSSST PSST
AND A FEW PUFFS THERE
PSSST

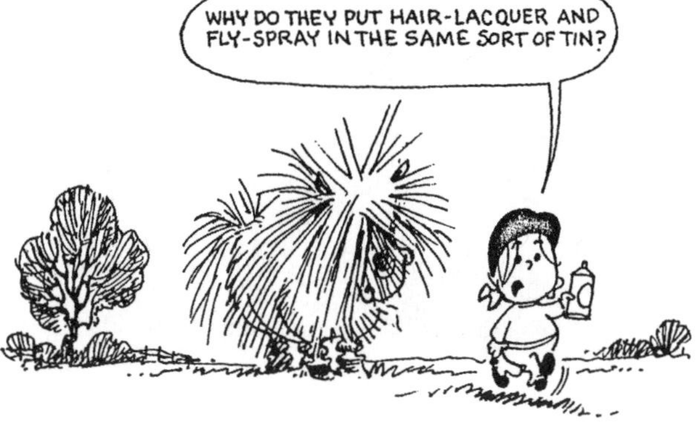
WHY DO THEY PUT HAIR-LACQUER AND FLY-SPRAY IN THE SAME SORT OF TIN?

IT'S NO USE TRYING TO ARGUE WITH KIPPER THIS MORNING
HE JUST DIGS HIS HEELS IN!
LET ME TRY!
WHAT'S ALL THE FUSS AND BOTHER ABOUT THEN?
I TOLD YOU HE'D DIG HIS HEELS IN!

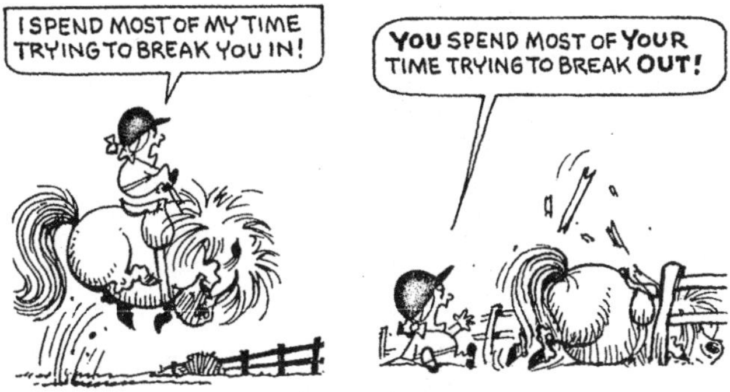
I SPEND MOST OF MY TIME TRYING TO BREAK YOU IN!
YOU SPEND MOST OF YOUR TIME TRYING TO BREAK OUT!

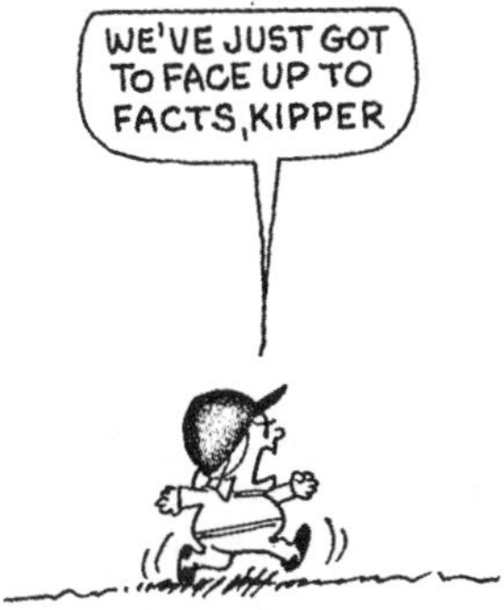
WE'VE JUST GOT TO FACE UP TO FACTS, KIPPER

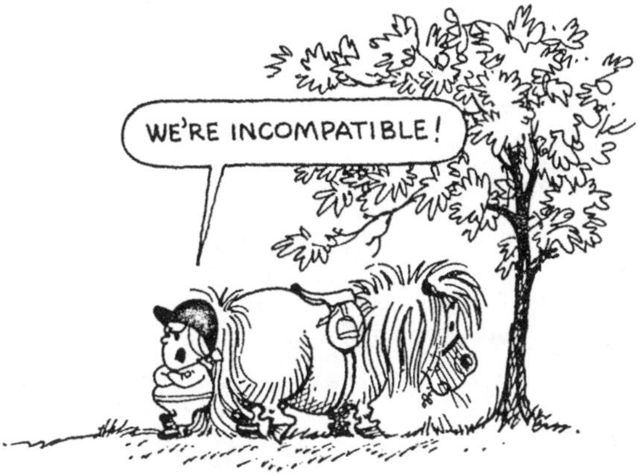
WE'RE INCOMPATIBLE!

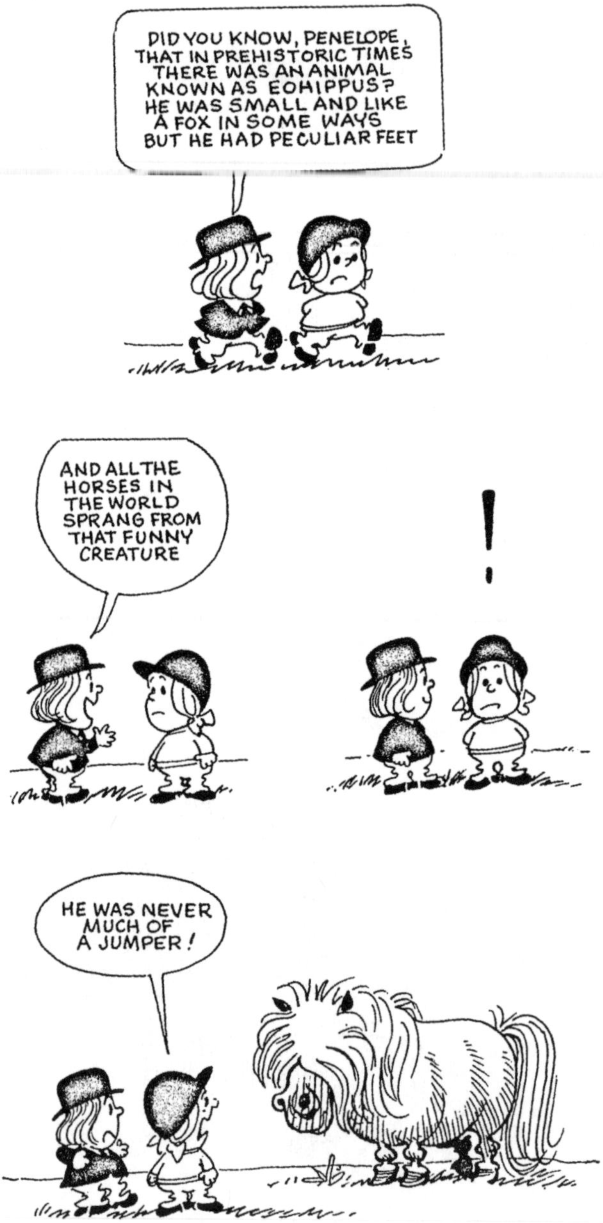
DID YOU KNOW, PENELOPE, THAT IN PREHISTORIC TIMES THERE WAS AN ANIMAL KNOWN AS EOHIPPUS? HE WAS SMALL AND LIKE A FOX IN SOME WAYS BUT HE HAD PECULIAR FEET
AND ALL THE HORSES IN THE WORLD SPRANG FROM THAT FUNNY CREATURE
!
HE WAS NEVER MUCH OF A JUMPER!

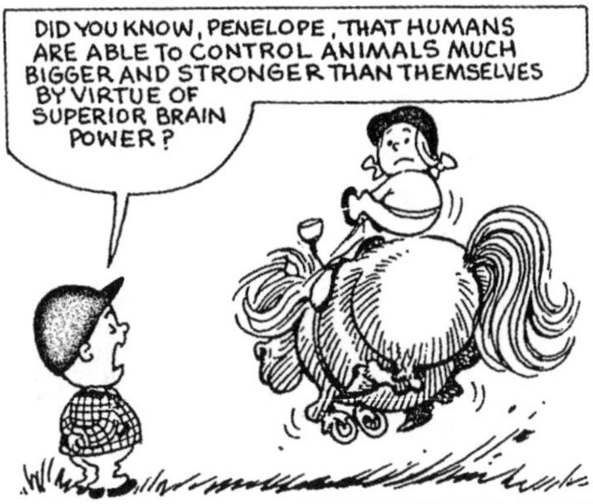
DID YOU KNOW, PENELOPE, THAT HUMANS ARE ABLE TO CONTROL ANIMALS MUCH BIGGER AND STRONGER THAN THEMSELVES BY VIRTUE OF SUPERIOR BRAIN POWER?

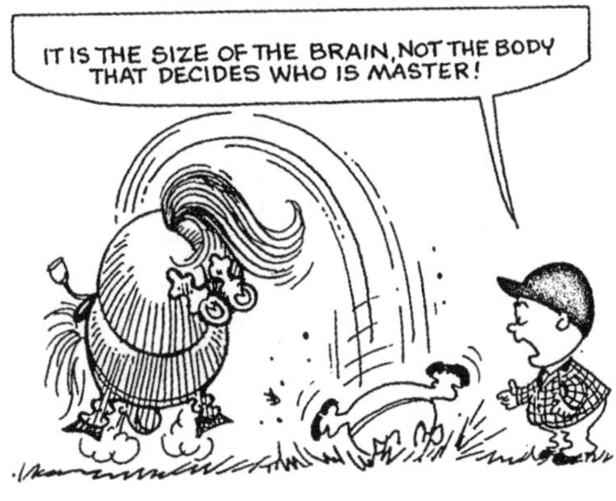
IT IS THE SIZE OF THE BRAIN, NOT THE BODY THAT DECIDES WHO IS MASTER!

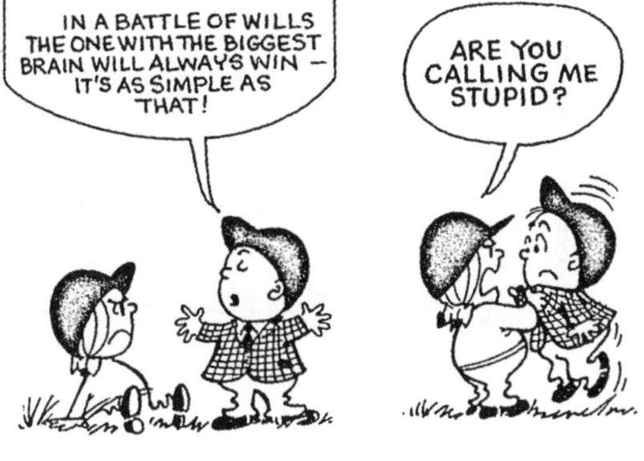
IN A BATTLE OF WILLS THE ONE WITH THE BIGGEST BRAIN WILL ALWAYS WIN — IT'S AS SIMPLE AS THAT!
ARE YOU CALLING ME STUPID?

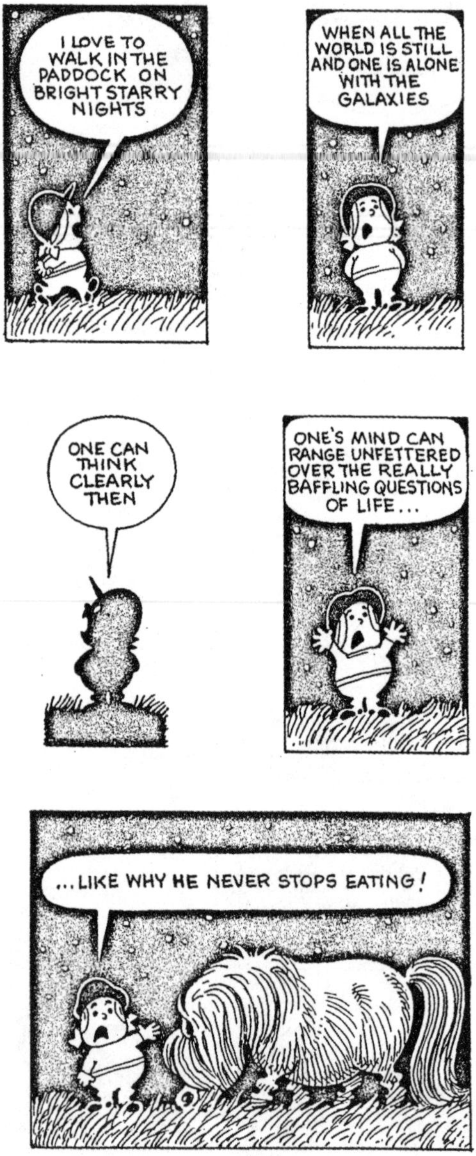
I LOVE TO WALK IN THE PADDOCK ON BRIGHT STARRY NIGHTS
WHEN ALL THE WORLD IS STILL AND ONE IS ALONE WITH THE GALAXIES
ONE CAN THINK CLEARLY THEN
ONE'S MIND CAN RANGE UNFETTERED OVER THE REALLY BAFFLING QUESTIONS OF LIFE...
...LIKE WHY HE NEVER STOPS EATING!

YOU'RE A BAD, BAD PONY!
WHAT DID HE DO, PENELOPE?
WHAT DID HE DO? HE WENT FOR A TRAMP IN LONG-MEADOW. THAT'S WHAT HE DID!
WHAT'S SO BAD ABOUT THAT?
HE TORE A BIG PIECE OUT OF THE POOR MAN'S TROUSERS

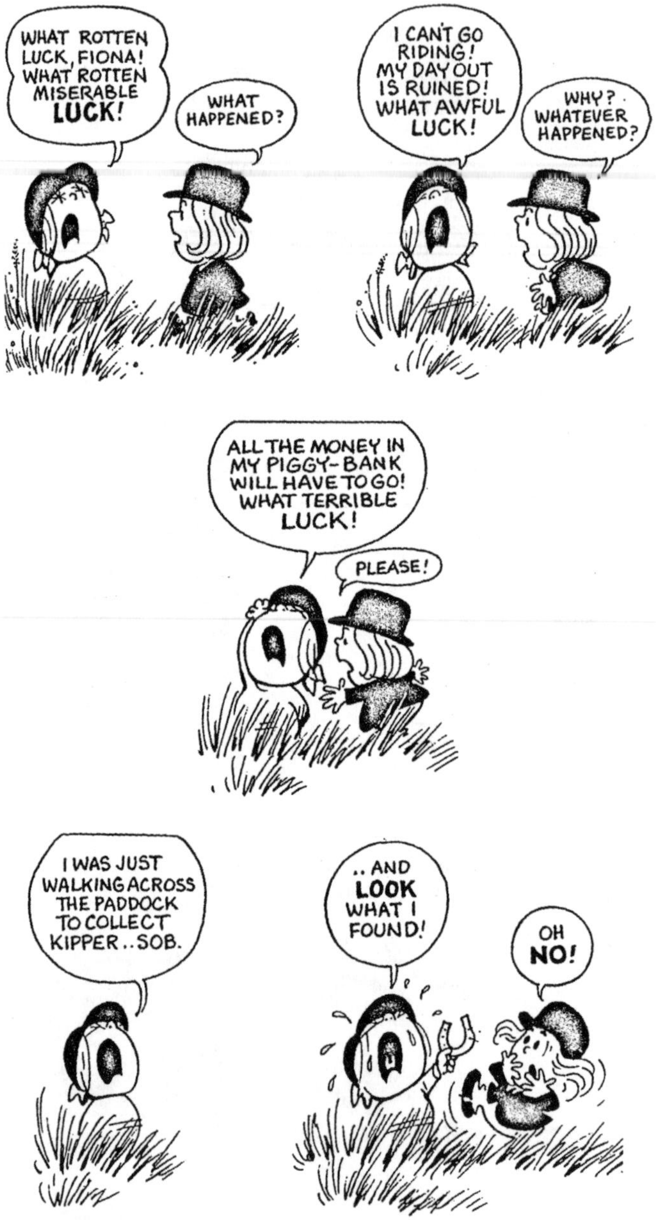
WHAT ROTTEN LUCK, FIONA! WHAT ROTTEN MISERABLE LUCK!
WHAT HAPPENED?
I CAN'T GO RIDING! MY DAY OUT IS RUINED! WHAT AWFUL LUCK!
WHY? WHATEVER HAPPENED?
ALL THE MONEY IN MY PIGGY-BANK WILL HAVE TO GO! WHAT TERRIBLE LUCK!
PLEASE!
I WAS JUST WALKING ACROSS THE PADDOCK TO COLLECT KIPPER.. SOB.
.. AND LOOK WHAT I FOUND!
OH NO!

IF YOU DON'T GET UP I'LL THUMP YOU!
PENELOPE! HOLD IT YOU MUSTN'T STRIKE KIPPER!
WHY NOT? HE DRIVES ME CRAZY!
BECAUSE POOR OLD KIPPER DOESN'T UNDERSTAND HOW YOU FEEL!
DO YOU UNDERSTAND HOW I FEEL, MAGNUS?
YES OF COURSE I DO!
BONK!
WHAT DID I SAY?

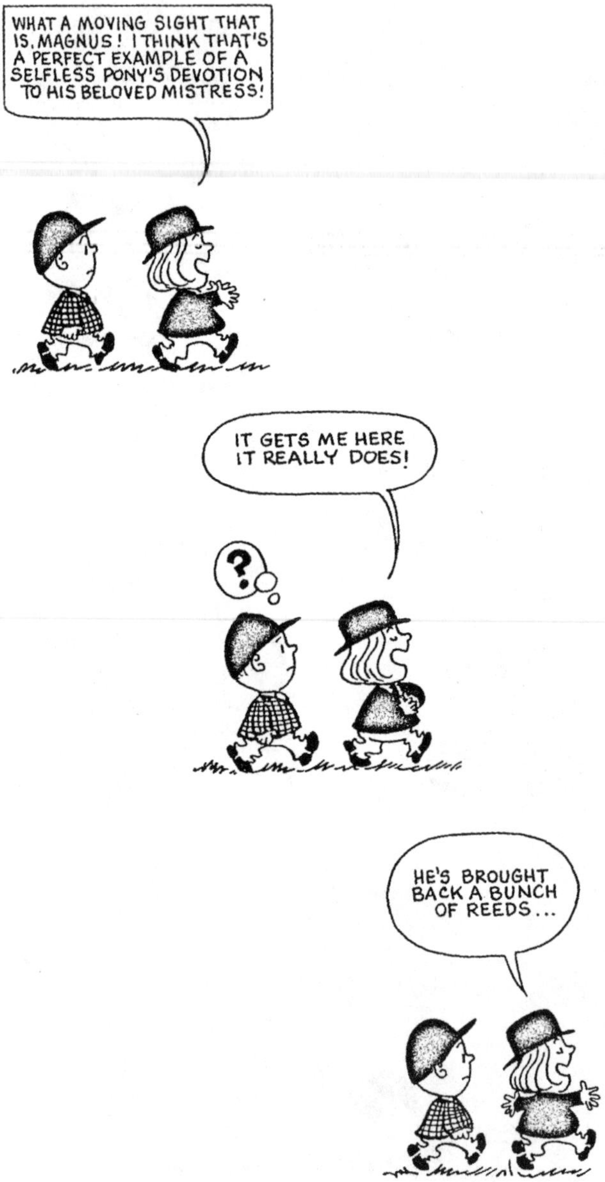
WHAT A MOVING SIGHT THAT IS, MAGNUS! I THINK THAT'S A PERFECT EXAMPLE OF A SELFLESS PONY'S DEVOTION TO HIS BELOVED MISTRESS!
IT GETS ME HERE IT REALLY DOES!
?
HE'S BROUGHT BACK A BUNCH OF REEDS...

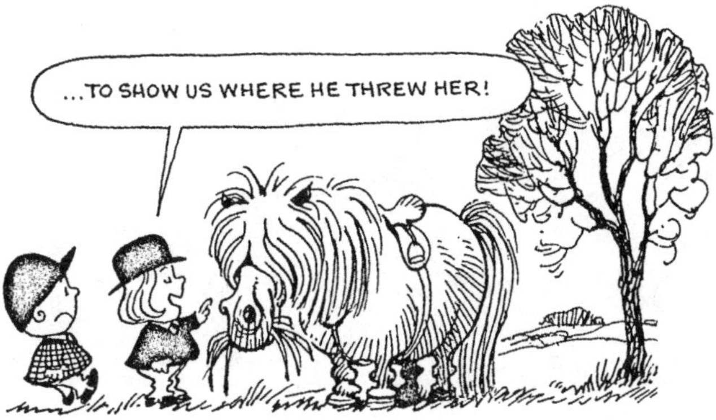
...TO SHOW US WHERE HE THREW HER!

WOULD YOU LIKE A PIECE, PENELOPE ?
INTO THE DITCH QUICK!
CRACKLE!
CRACKLE!
CRACKLE!
CRACKLE!
CRACKLE!
CRACKLE!
YOU KNOW HE CAN HEAR A CHOCOLATE WRAPPER FROM THREE FIELDS AWAY!

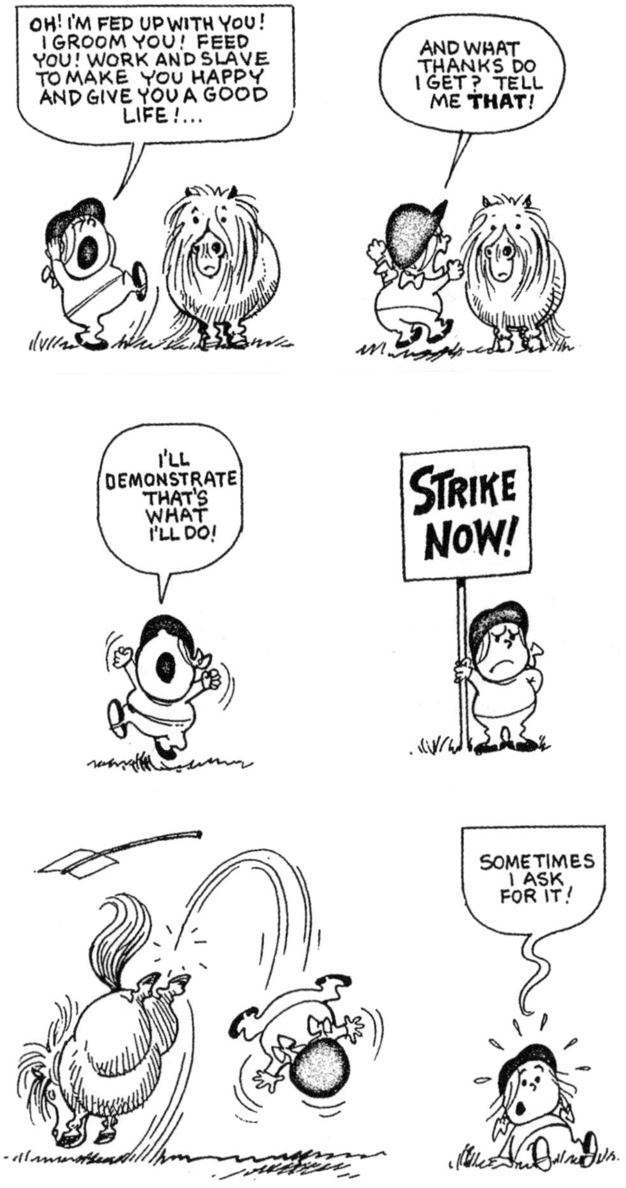
OH! I'M FED UP WITH YOU! I GROOM YOU! FEED YOU! WORK AND SLAVE TO MAKE YOU HAPPY AND GIVE YOU A GOOD LIFE!...
AND WHAT THANKS DO I GET? TELL ME THAT!
I'LL DEMONSTRATE THAT'S WHAT I'LL DO!
STRIKE NOW!
SOMETIMES I ASK FOR IT!

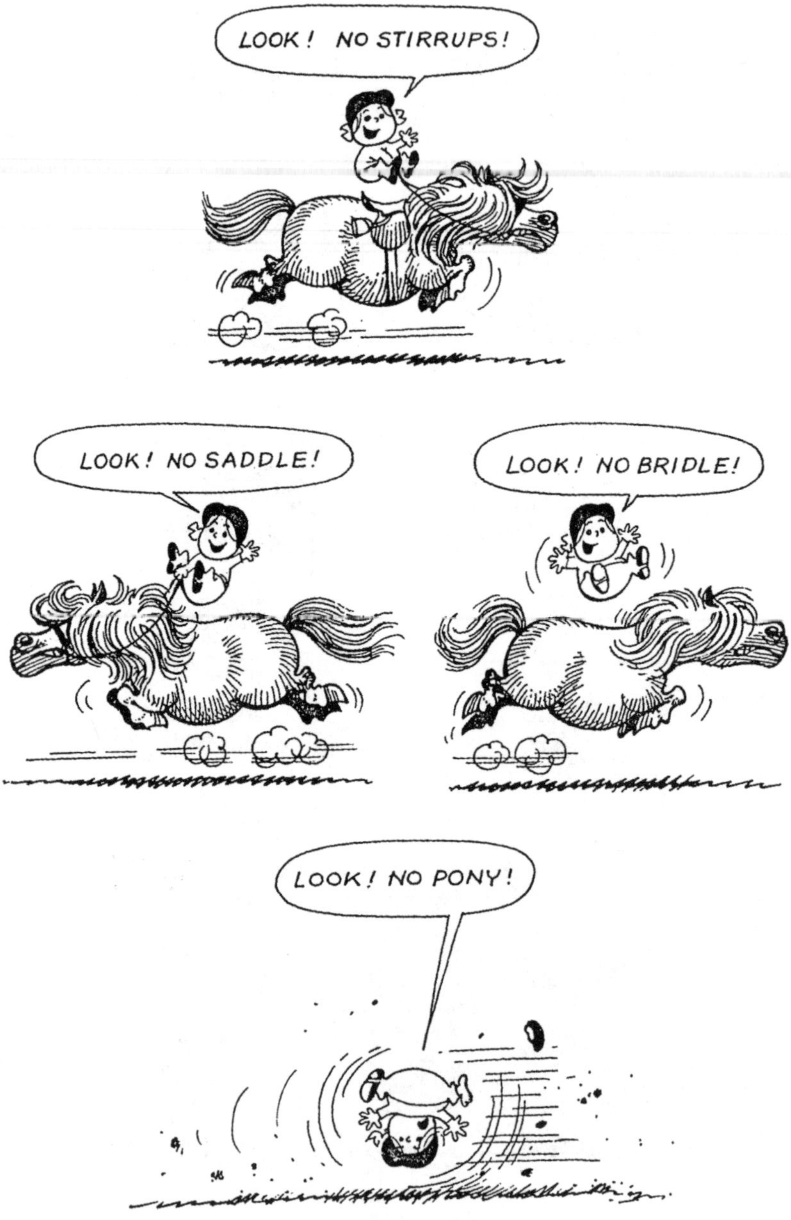
LOOK! NO STIRRUPS!
LOOK! NO SADDLE!
LOOK! NO BRIDLE!
LOOK! NO PONY!

PEOPLE ARE ALWAYS ASKING ME WHY I RIDE
'WHY DO YOU TAKE THE RISKS' THEY SAY. 'WHAT DO YOU GET OUT OF IT?'
THEY'RE DIFFICULT QUESTIONS TO ANSWER
I SUPPOSE I JUST DO IT FOR KICKS!

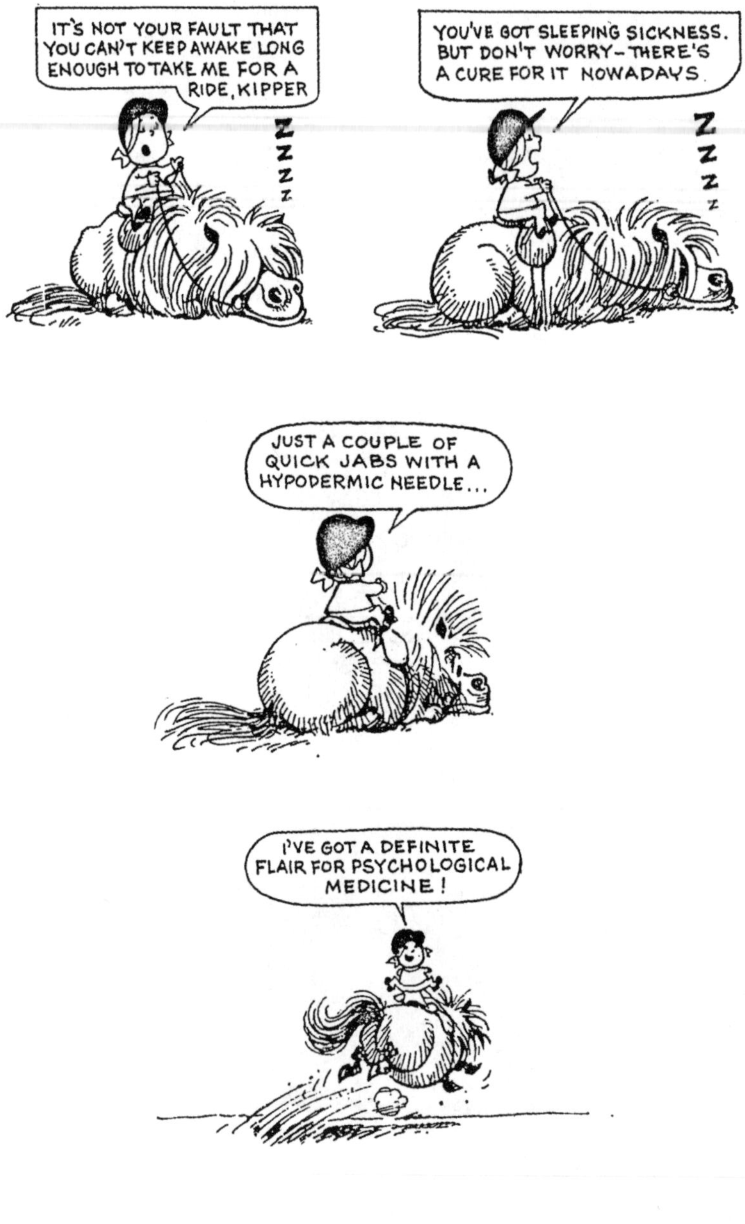
IT'S NOT YOUR FAULT THAT YOU CAN'T KEEP AWAKE LONG ENOUGH TO TAKE ME FOR A RIDE, KIPPER
Z Z Z Z
YOU'VE GOT SLEEPING SICKNESS. BUT DON'T WORRY – THERE'S A CURE FOR IT NOWADAYS.
Z Z Z Z
JUST A COUPLE OF QUICK JABS WITH A HYPODERMIC NEEDLE...
I'VE GOT A DEFINITE FLAIR FOR PSYCHOLOGICAL MEDICINE!

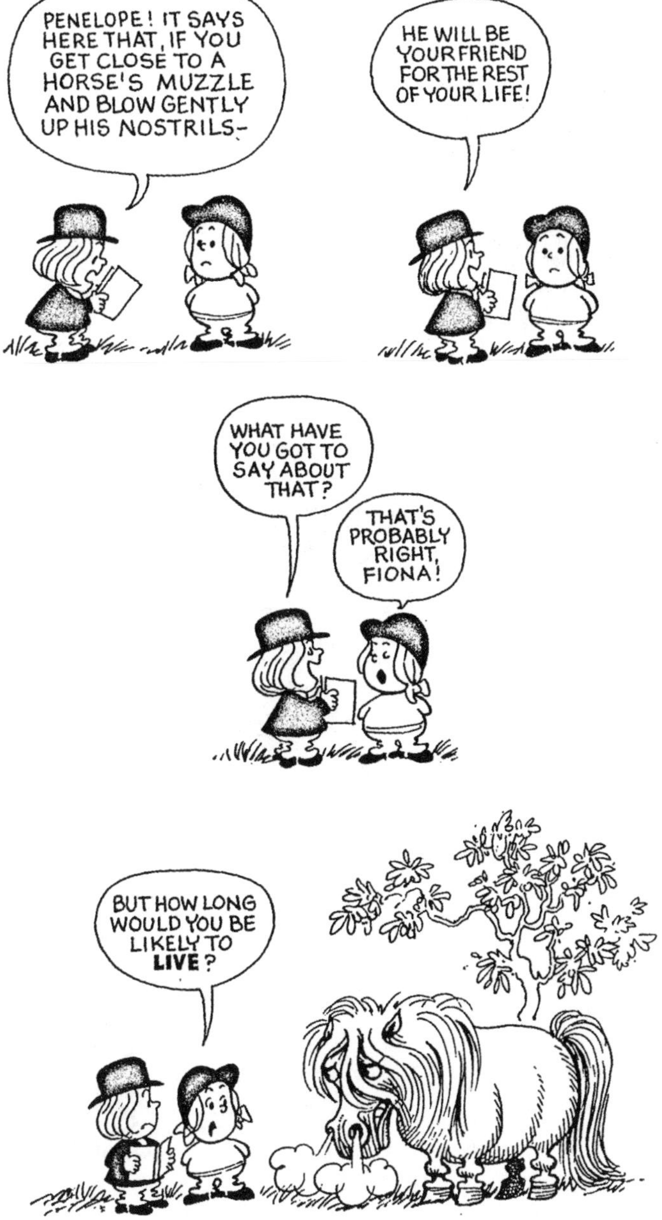
PENELOPE! IT SAYS HERE THAT, IF YOU GET CLOSE TO A HORSE'S MUZZLE AND BLOW GENTLY UP HIS NOSTRILS-
HE WILL BE YOUR FRIEND FOR THE REST OF YOUR LIFE!
WHAT HAVE YOU GOT TO SAY ABOUT THAT?
THAT'S PROBABLY RIGHT, FIONA!
BUT HOW LONG WOULD YOU BE LIKELY TO **LIVE**?

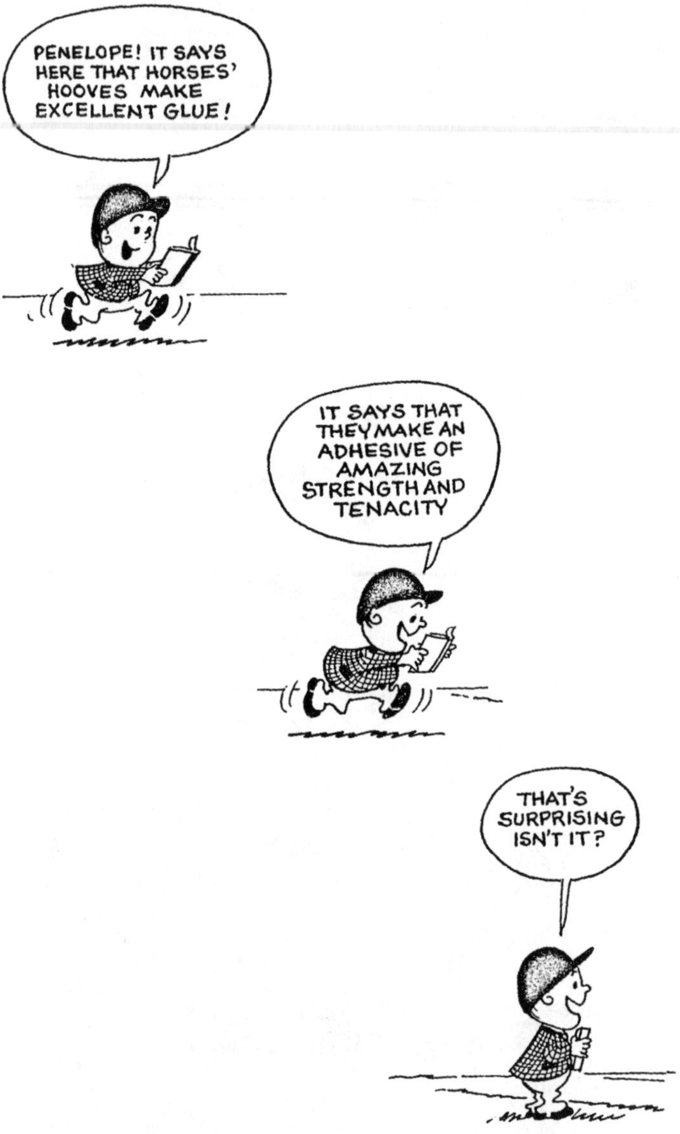
PENELOPE! IT SAYS HERE THAT HORSES' HOOVES MAKE EXCELLENT GLUE!
IT SAYS THAT THEY MAKE AN ADHESIVE OF AMAZING STRENGTH AND TENACITY
THAT'S SURPRISING ISN'T IT?

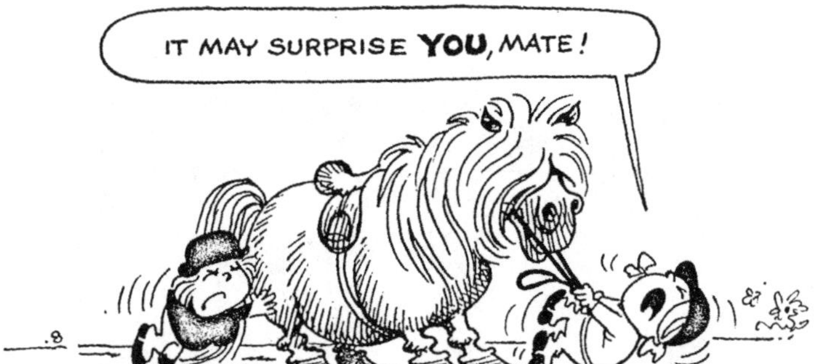
IT MAY SURPRISE YOU, MATE!

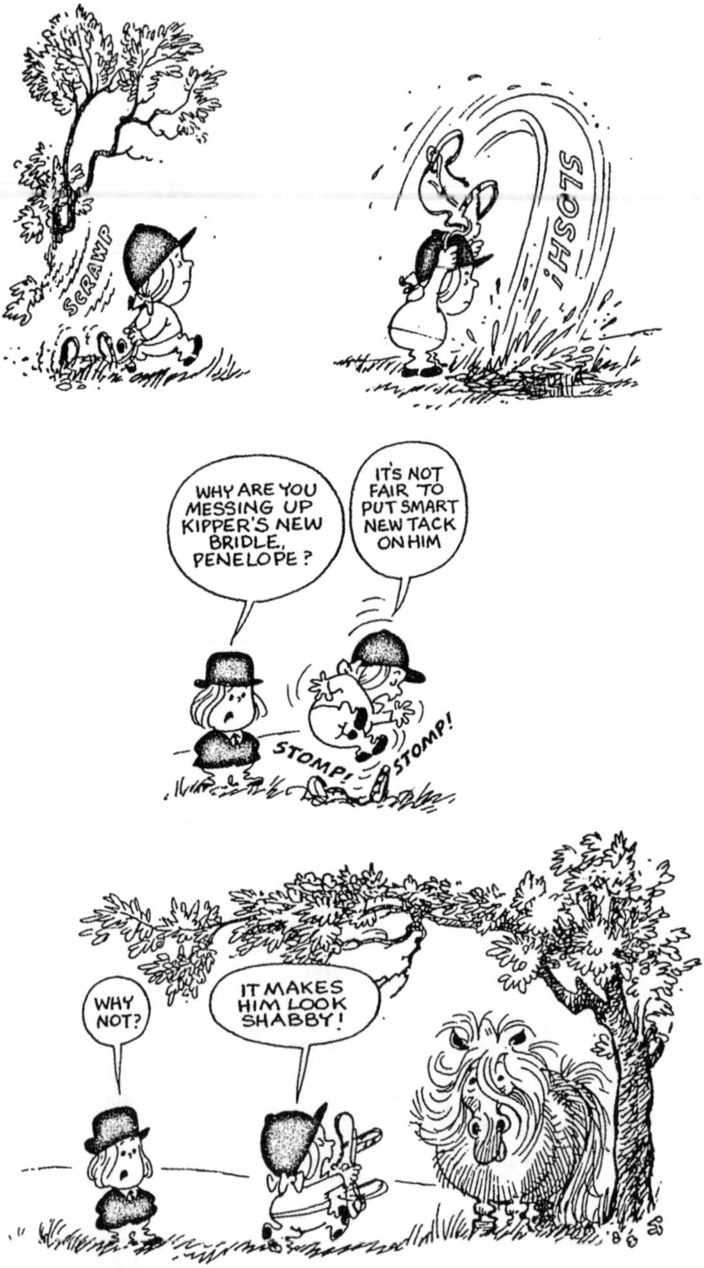
SCRAWP
SLOSH!
WHY ARE YOU MESSING UP KIPPER'S NEW BRIDLE, PENELOPE?
IT'S NOT FAIR TO PUT SMART NEW TACK ON HIM
STOMP!
STOMP!
WHY NOT?
IT MAKES HIM LOOK SHABBY!

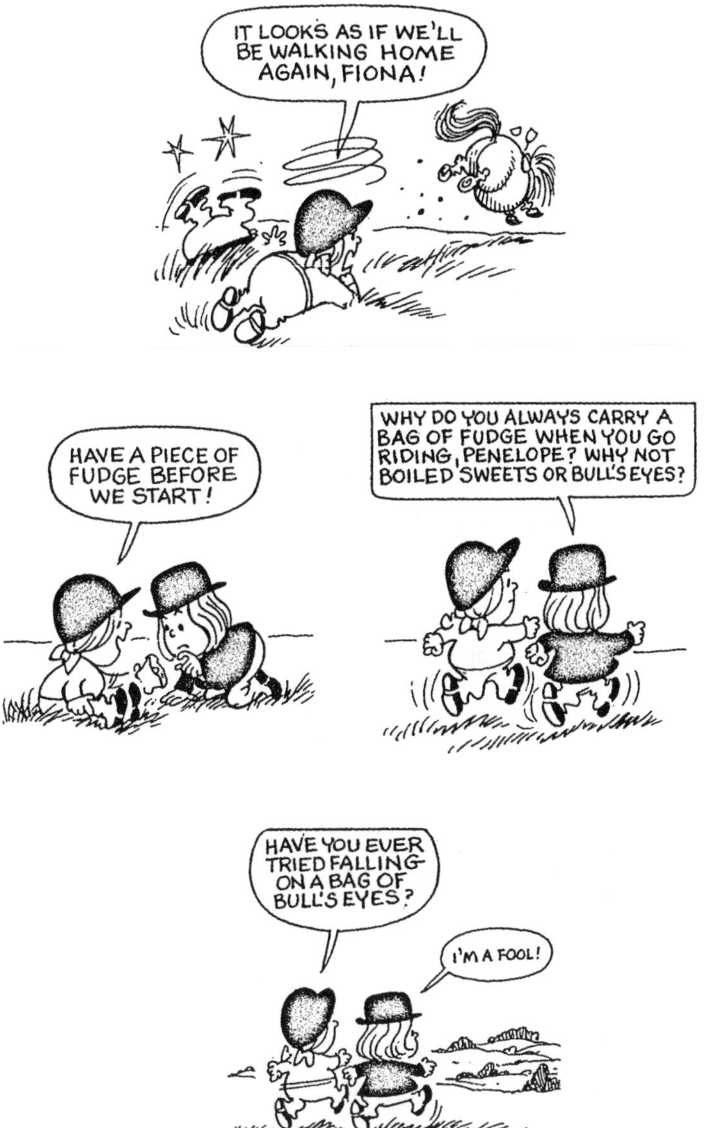
IT LOOKS AS IF WE'LL BE WALKING HOME AGAIN, FIONA!
HAVE A PIECE OF FUDGE BEFORE WE START!
WHY DO YOU ALWAYS CARRY A BAG OF FUDGE WHEN YOU GO RIDING, PENELOPE? WHY NOT BOILED SWEETS OR BULL'S EYES?
HAVE YOU EVER TRIED FALLING ON A BAG OF BULL'S EYES?
I'M A FOOL!

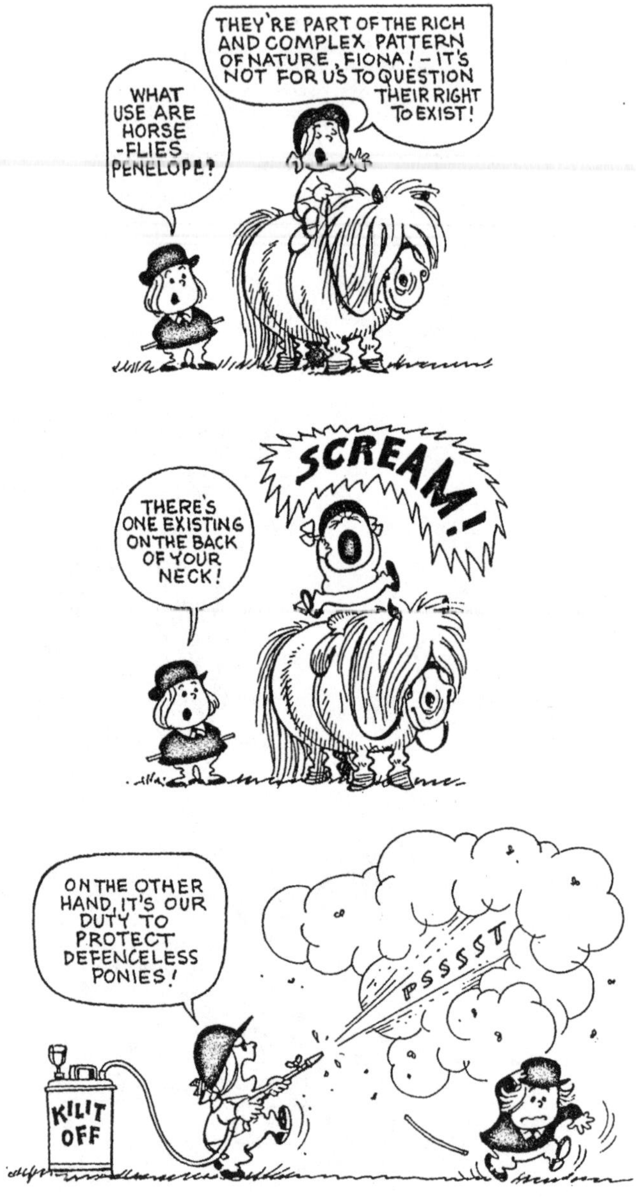
WHAT USE ARE HORSE -FLIES PENELOPE?
THEY'RE PART OF THE RICH AND COMPLEX PATTERN OF NATURE, FIONA! – IT'S NOT FOR US TO QUESTION THEIR RIGHT TO EXIST!
THERE'S ONE EXISTING ON THE BACK OF YOUR NECK!
SCREAM!
ON THE OTHER HAND, IT'S OUR DUTY TO PROTECT DEFENCELESS PONIES!
KILIT OFF
PSSSST

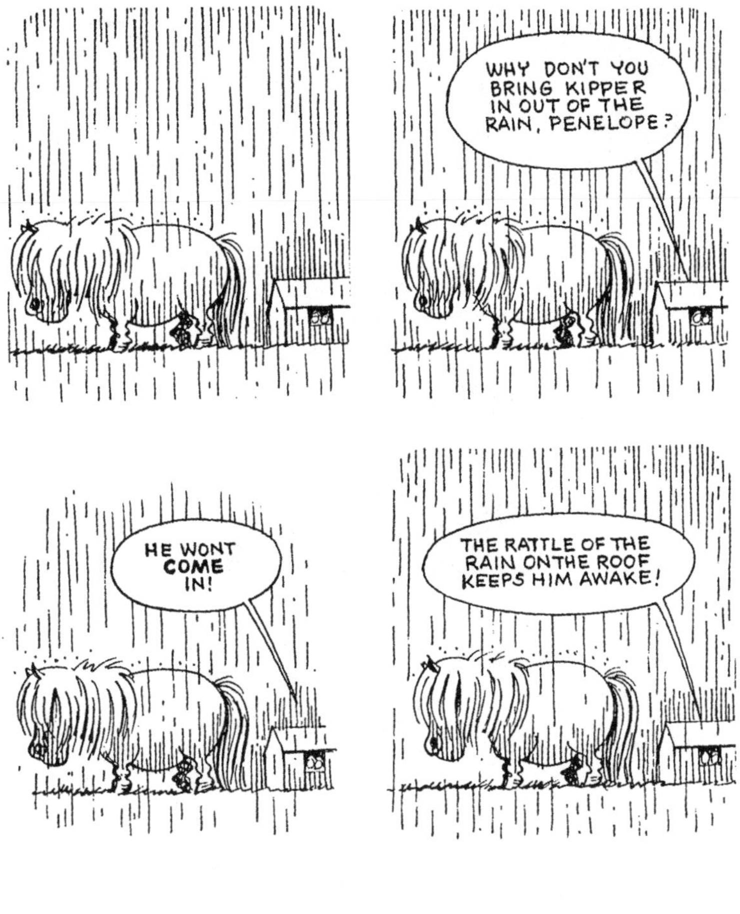
WHY DON'T YOU BRING KIPPER IN OUT OF THE RAIN, PENELOPE?
HE WONT COME IN!
THE RATTLE OF THE RAIN ON THE ROOF KEEPS HIM AWAKE!

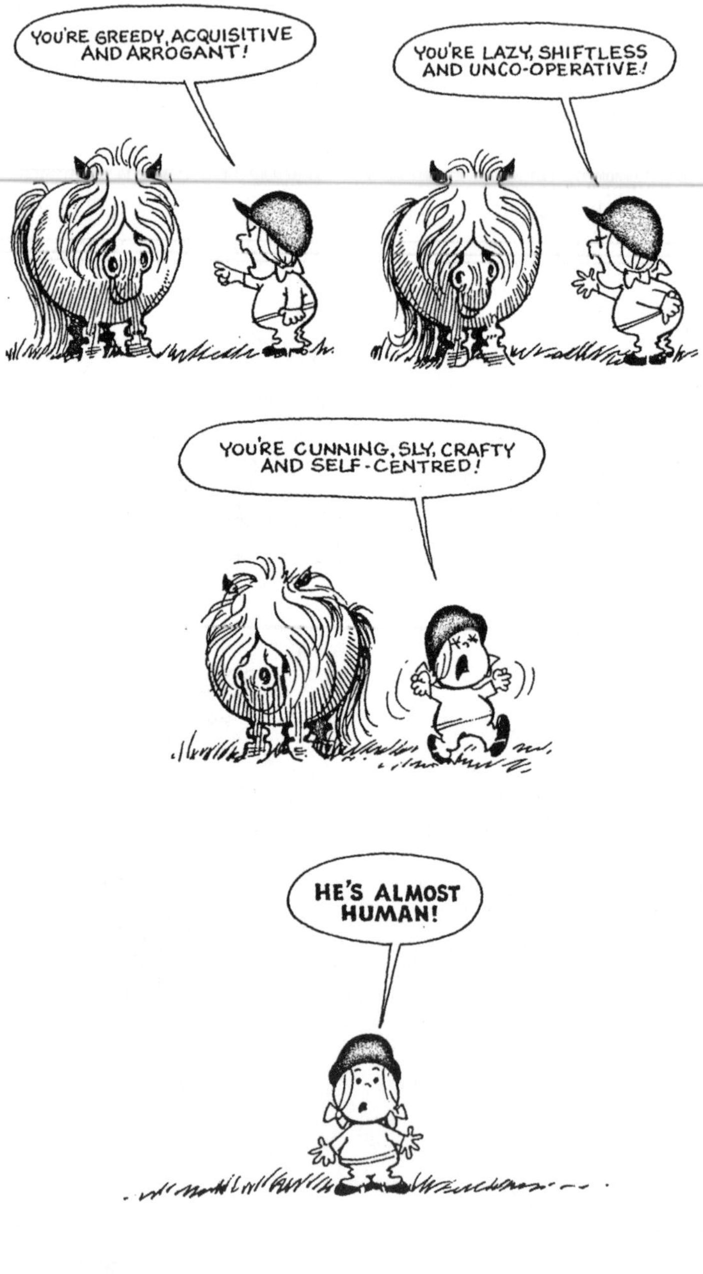
YOU'RE GREEDY, ACQUISITIVE AND ARROGANT!
YOU'RE LAZY, SHIFTLESS AND UNCO-OPERATIVE!
YOU'RE CUNNING, SLY, CRAFTY AND SELF-CENTRED!
HE'S ALMOST HUMAN!

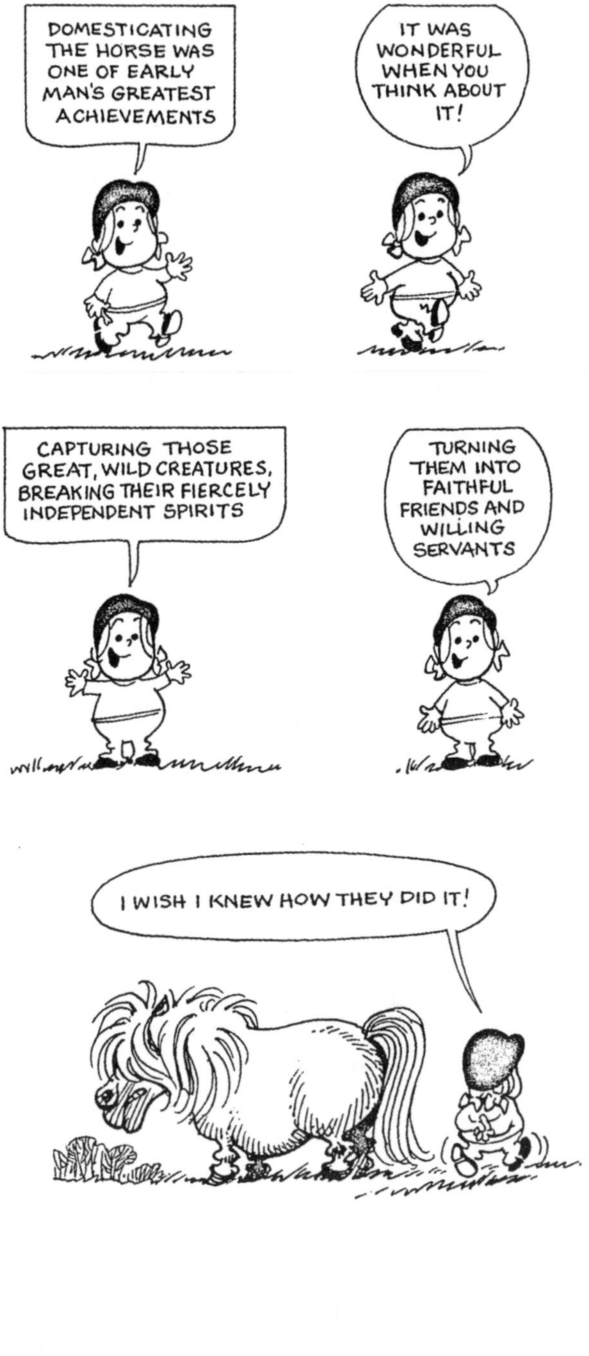
DOMESTICATING THE HORSE WAS ONE OF EARLY MAN'S GREATEST ACHIEVEMENTS
IT WAS WONDERFUL WHEN YOU THINK ABOUT IT!
CAPTURING THOSE GREAT, WILD CREATURES, BREAKING THEIR FIERCELY INDEPENDENT SPIRITS
TURNING THEM INTO FAITHFUL FRIENDS AND WILLING SERVANTS
I WISH I KNEW HOW THEY DID IT!

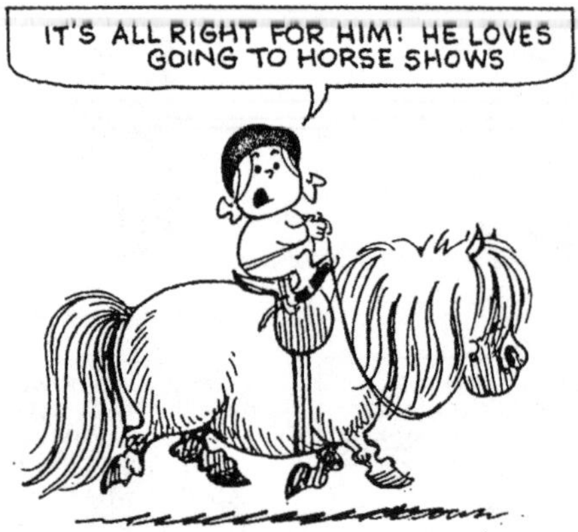
IT'S ALL RIGHT FOR HIM! HE LOVES GOING TO HORSE SHOWS

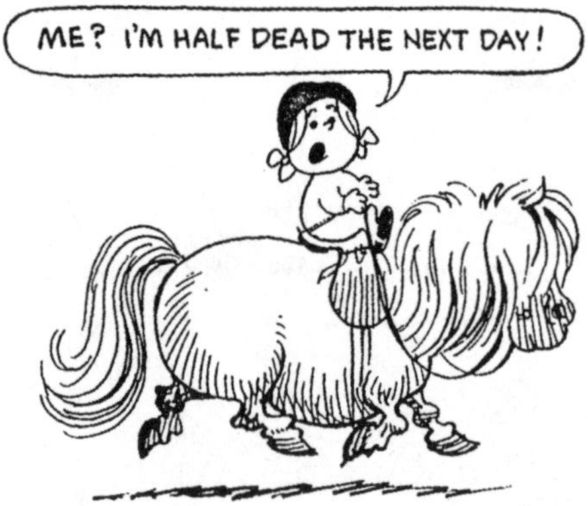
ME? I'M HALF DEAD THE NEXT DAY!

WHY ARE YOU ALWAYS BELTING UP AND DOWN ON A PONY, PENELOPE?
I HAVE TO DO SOMETHING TO KEEP MYSELF FIT!
FIT FOR WHAT?
FOR BELTING UP AND DOWN ON A PONY OF COURSE, STUPID!